THE FIRST FIVE

A LOVE LETTER TO TEACHERS

PATRICK HARRIS II

FOREWORD BY **CHEZARE A. WARREN**

HEINEMANN
Portsmouth, NH

Heinemann
145 Maplewood Avenue, Suite 300
Portsmouth, NH 03801
www.heinemann.com

Heinemann's authors have devoted their entire careers to developing the unique content in their works, and their written expression is protected by copyright law. We respectfully ask that you do not adapt, reuse, or copy anything on third-party (whether for-profit or not-for-profit) lesson-sharing websites.

—Heinemann Publishers

"Dedicated to Teachers" is a trademark of Greenwood Publishing Group, LLC.

The author and publisher wish to thank those who have generously given permission to reprint borrowed material:

p. 5: © Globe Turner, LLC/Getty Images; p. 25: © Rita Baros/Getty Images; p. 29: © CRS PHOTO/Shutterstock; p. 31: © Patrick A. Burns/New York Times Co./Getty Images; p. 33: © Amy Sussman/WireImage/Getty Images; pp. 54–55: The Reading Room/Alamy; p. 75: © Pertusina/Shutterstock; pp. 86–87: © anildash/Shutterstock; pp. 88–89: © Nico Traut/Shutterstock; p. 105: © Debra Reschoff Ahearn/Dreamstime; p. 111: © Samuel Corum/Anadolu Agency/Getty Images; © AP Photo/Manuel Balce Ceneta.

Library of Congress Control Number: 2022931580
ISBN: 978-0-325-13695-0

Editor: Holly Kim Price
Production: Vicki Kasabian
Cover and text designs: Monica Ann Cohen
Typesetting: Monica Ann Cohen
Manufacturing: Val Cooper

Printed in the United States of America on acid-free paper
2 3 4 5 MP 26 25 24 23 22   PO 34805

TO MY YOUNGER SELF,

WAY AHEAD OF HIS TIME,

TOO IN THE RACE TO STOP FOR THE LESSONS.

AND FOR ALL THOSE WHO ANSWER

THE CALL TO TEACH.

CONTENTS

FOREWORD

LOVE IS AN ACTION WORD. AN INTENTION. A COMMITMENT. TO LOVE IS TO HONOR BOTH the good and the bad, the beautiful and the unsightly. Loving necessitates some suffering, but the object of deep affection is deserving and worthy of the best we have to offer no matter how arduous the love journey. And it is a journey. Giving, pouring, and sacrificing of oneself in service to their own or someone else's healing and well-being constitutes the highest form of impenitent benevolence. Love rewards us with countless life lessons if we allow it to, even when those lessons invite regret and lament.

What you hold in your hand (or are viewing on your screen) is the product of Patrick Harris' boundless love. His love of self despite coming of age in an anti-Black, racist, homophobic world. His love of young people and the twinkle of their inherent brilliance. His love for the embattled and woefully undervalued profession of teaching. And, most pointedly, his love for teachers. Yes! Those individuals brave enough to occupy the front lines of education, who do their jobs with deftness despite the deafening noise of an uninformed public discourse about teaching in the digital age. From the first story Patrick tells, to the questions of reflection he poses to the community of voices included in this epic love letter, it is clear that he loves teachers and teaching.

And so, in the spirit of *The First Five*, I will narrate a small part of my own love journey to teaching and becoming a teacher. This book involuntarily thrust me back in time to the 1980s—to my childhood in Chicago about four hours from Detroit where Patrick grew up. Marge was our next-door neighbor and babysitter. I can remember sitting in her basement boisterously gathering the two-, three-, and four-year-olds to teach them the ABCs, exuberantly sharing what I learned just days before. Even from such a young age, I loved the project of knowledge exchange. In fifth grade, I'd create handwritten worksheets for other kids to complete based on something we'd studied the week before. In middle school and high school, I volunteered for any role that positioned me to prepare my classmates to learn a specific skill or complete a task.

I graduated from my state's flagship institution of higher education with a degree in elementary education in a program identical to the one Patrick completed, poised to change the world teaching Black kids back home on Chicago's west and south sides. But also, like Patrick, I became disheartened by the many obstacles to doing the one thing that I've always loved to do. The lack of expansive representations of blackness and Black people in the curriculum. The incessant focus on raising test scores no matter how much drill and (s)kill. The insistence that I place discipline in my classroom above student care, joy, and agency. It was all so unsettling. I, like Patrick, began changing schools to find the perfect set of working conditions. Five schools in five years. There were so many questions brewing in my mind about if I could retire from a career as a K–12 educator. I wondered what it would take to change teaching for the better. I pondered what role I might play to effect real change for kids, families, and colleagues.

To answer many of the questions bumping up against long-held beliefs about teaching in my head, I went to graduate school. Patrick went to Twitter. Two of us on parallel journeys across time and space with a few twists and turns that led our paths to intersect at Michigan State University (MSU). Here I am, a first-year assistant professor of teacher education, encountering a young Black man from "the city" like me doing the same exact thing I was doing a decade before him. I did not know, however, that the undergraduate student speaker at my first MSU commencement would go on to craft such an extraordinary set of professional experiences—pivotal moments, incidences, and interactions that would lead to publication of this must-read extended playlist of chapters melodically narrating Patrick's first five years in our beloved profession.

I could not stop smiling as I read *The First Five*, and you won't either. Patrick uses every page of this book to articulate wisdoms that I have long struggled to comprehend, even with my decade of expertise as an education researcher. Doing and being are not in opposition. In other words, doing the work of teaching and being a teacher, while symbiotic, are indeed mutually exclusive exercises. I loved teaching, but I grew to lament being a teacher. My discontent with being a teacher was in many ways because I was too often distracted from remembering my why. I did not have enough reminders of the love of teaching that brought me to the profession in the first place. It is this love that indeed sustains me in my present role as a university faculty member.

The First Five is an unabashed offering of solidarity to teachers, and a reminder to love themselves enough to tell the truth about what it takes to do this vital work with youth and young people. This book names the complexities of the job with clarity and candor. Patrick uses his experience as a witty case study through which to discern how we might build an education ecosystem that foremost appreciates the difficulty of teaching. This book is both a retrospective and a road map. Patrick is still in the classroom. In a voice all his own, Patrick also uses *The First Five* to emphasize the pride in being a teacher. This book is the intervention I needed as a young teacher to help me know I was not alone. I needed to be reminded that what I was feeling was valid, and that this journey would take me to heights (and depths) unknown if I just remembered to lean into the love above and against everything else.

The First Five is, in Patrick's words, a "love letter to teachers." It evokes all the emotions and titillates the senses. You have a front row seat to Patrick's journey of love, which also means you get the privilege of witnessing both his grief and his joy. Behold his revelation and his confusion as he navigates six schools in five years. The beautiful images and story-telling style are icing on the cake, making for a lavish adventure into Patrick's inner self. There are no dull moments. I hope Patrick's journey of love points you toward the healing and wholeness we all deserve—teacher or not. This is his love letter. A gift to pass along for many years to come, from him to all of us.

— Chezare A. Warren, Vanderbilt University

ACKNOWLEDGMENTS

I WOULD LIKE TO THANK . . .

. . . THE ACADEMY. HAHA. I'M JUST KIDDING. LET ME BE SERIOUS. WRITING *THE FIRST Five* was terrifying. I talked myself out of writing this book more times than I'm ready to admit. There are more intelligent educators out there. There are better writers. There are people with far more experience and expertise. It's not my time yet. And yet, I answered the call anyway. Thankfully, I did not have to do it alone. I am so grateful for my people.

My journey writing this book began at the 2017 National Council of Teachers of English conference. In the Thursday evening general assembly to be exact. I'm not sure who the speaker was or what they said. But I felt it in my spirit to walk up to the microphone intending to ask a question, but instead ended up venting my frustrations about having to use a basal for reading instruction.

I thought it was important at the time to amplify the current challenges other teachers and I faced developing literacy experiences for kids. One-size-fits-all curriculums were one of them. I should've been nervous. But my adrenaline was pumping. The crowd erupted in applause. I fist-bumped so many teachers after that moment. I owe the biggest thank-you to Brett for finding me afterwards and uplifting me. Thank you to Cornelius for making time to pour into me in the middle of a hallway at the conference. This journey got its kick-start because both of you saw the potential in me, my voice, and my message before I saw it in myself.

Good writing happens because of good editing! But Holly, you are so much more than my trusted editor. You have truly been a second mom to me. When we first met, you just simply asked me what I was thinking about. You did not want me to rush an idea (and boy has it changed over time). Instead, you encouraged me to embrace the journey, even in all of its unpredictability and transience. You have been here through it all. Thank you for welcoming me in your home. For listening to my wild ideas. And whew, for tackling the book when it was 15,000 words over the limit. Thank you.

This book is a love letter to my family, too. Y'all saw the teacher in me at four years old and invested in my dream to be in front of a classroom. I'm not sure I've always been as detailed and honest about the experiences I've had on my teaching journey. Nonetheless, thank you for accepting me as I am and supporting me along the way. Mom, thank you for your "I'm so proud of you" messages, they always stuck with me. Dad, thank you for calling me and sharing words of wisdom. Nana and Granddad, thank you for sharing your story with me and helping me fact-check. Grandma Margaret and Grandma Mattie, I hope I made you proud. Kaelan, Moya, Dallan, and Charlie, you're up next. My bonus parents, aunts, uncle, cousins, it's always all love.

In 2017, I asked a kindergarten teacher on Instagram whom I thought was pretty down-to-earth to join me in starting the *Common Sense* podcast. We had no idea what we were doing (we were recording in the back of our closets), but 100,000 downloads later it's clear that choosing to share our experiences as new teachers in only ways that we could, resonated with educators across the world. You became more than a cohost; thank you for being my best friend, Antonia. So much of this book is informed by your advice and the books you put in my hands. You taught me a new way of writing when you shared Dr. Michelle Foster's book *Black Teachers on Teaching*. You have always been right by my side through every doubt and school change. This book would simply not be possible without you.

There were many moments where imposter syndrome stepped in. And just as it was about to take me out, my best friends were there to fight with me. Egypt, Emettra, Drae, Parnell, Salem, Brittany, and Airel. Thank you for gassing me up and never letting me quit. Thank you for reminding me what giving myself grace looks like. Stephon, the greatest love I know, thank you for holding me when I did not know how to keep going. Thank you for sharing in my excitement. So much of the love you've given me is woven into these pages.

I'm grateful for my mentors. My #EduColor family, you wouldn't leave me to believe that I was alone in this work. Gary, my fellow author and brother, thank you for your endless support and inspiration. It was instrumental in my first years of teaching. Dr. Warren, not only am I deeply appreciative that you are writing the foreword, but I am also grateful because you answered all my calls when I was seeking scholarship to help expand my ideas and affirmation. After working in six schools in seven years, I finally found the right school for me. I had to do tons of rewriting because I am in good company with colleagues that push me and whom I call mentors. Thank you, my Roeper family, for the many conversations on theory and reflections on teaching and allowing me to be myself.

I knew when writing this that I was not the only educator with reflections and experiences that would resonate. I was inspired by Dr. Michelle Foster's work and so I conducted over fifteen interviews with teachers across the country and a few internationally. Unfortunately, not all of them were able to make the final copy of the book. I am still grateful for your stories and vulnerability. The essence of your stories still made a world of difference when writing.

Most of all, I thank every school and student that took a chance on me. From DC to Doha to Detroit. One of my current students suggested I should just make a list of all the students I've taught over the years, but I'm way over word count. My commitment to this profession is because of *all* of you. My hope comes from you. I would not be the person I am today without the love from all 203 of you. I hope I have made you proud. Keep telling your own stories; the world needs to hear them.

And to you. Every reader that picks up the book. I am deeply grateful. Thank you for taking the time to relive the journey that has been my first five years of teaching. Everyone's journey is different, but I know the power of storytelling builds bridges for us to do this work together. I hope this book inspires you to begin documenting and proudly sharing your own stories. This is the key to staying engaged in our human work.

INTRODUCTION

THE WEIGHT

Patrick, Not Pat :)
@PresidentPat

Thursday I'll officially be an Education major again and for the last time. No more changing!

Oct 23, 2011

I HUGGED MY MOM IN THE CAR AND RAN INTO THE BACK ENTRANCE OF MICHIGAN STATE University's Breslin Center. This was one of the few times I had ever stepped foot inside the basketball arena. I switched between an energetic sprint and a slow skip, moving my way through the crowd. One hand holding my green cap and the other bunching my gown to keep me from tripping and falling but still being careful not to mess up my nana's carefully ironed crease.

The march from the curtain to the stage was euphoric. It was an out-of-body experience. I didn't hear the music or the crowd roaring. All I could feel were the hairs raising on my arm and the butterflies gathering. My four years flashed before me with each step toward the stage.

I was chosen to give one of two "senior responses" during my college commencement. It was the ultimate thank-you to my family for their unwavering support over the last four years. Being the first to do anything comes with a lot of pressure. And while your family wants to help, they may struggle to find the words or offer advice because

"AT ORIENTATION, MY **MIND** WAS **CONSUMED BY THE ADVICE** I WAS GIVEN AND THE ARTICLES I HAD READ THAT SAID **TEACHING WAS NOT THE PROFESSION** TO ENTER. THEY TOLD ME TO **DREAM BIGGER.** BUT AS I MANEUVERED THROUGH MY FIRST YEAR OF COLLEGE, I HAD MANY **OPPORTUNITIES** KNOCKING ON MY DOOR AND EACH AND **EVERY ONE OF THEM** LEAD ME TO WORKING BACK WITH KIDS. AND SO FROM THIS, I HAVE LEARNED THAT **WHEN YOU HAVE A CALLING IN LIFE. PICK UP."**

—COMMENCEMENT SPEECH 2015

it's a foreign experience. Despite not having gone to college themselves, my support system still found ways to help me navigate this new world. This was our moment, our time.

I was a Black man speaking in front of the College of Education. The demographic of the graduating class studying education closely reflected the profession's demographic. I was one of a handful of Black students in the college and the only Black male educator in my program.

I'm not sure what brought on the tears first. It might have been being able to laser focus on my mom in the crowd, seeing her wipe her tears. Or it may have been seeing my nana alongside my now 102-year-old great-grandmother and recognizing the magnitude of this moment for our family. It might have been my siblings, some whom have never met one another, blending together. My dad and my grandfather's proud gaze. It might have been hearing the piercing *alright*s and elongated *yessss* from familiar Black voices in the audience. The tears came running without warning at the podium. And with each step I took back to my seat, I was reassured that I was exactly where I needed to be.

When I walked off that stage, I would prepare to start my teaching career carrying an immense amount of weight. I was feeling the heaviness of educational inequity for people who looked like me. Considering Black men are just less than 2 percent of the teaching force, the unicorns of the profession, I knew both the privilege and the pressure. It would be both an honor and a responsibility to answer the call. I was carrying Michael Brown's murder and the protests that followed. There was pressure building; the pressure of my queerness inside of me just waiting to be released. The pressure of perfectionism, not wanting to let down my family or my future students or myself. Knowing when I graduated college, I

would begin living my life out and proud. Still considering that the Gay, Lesbian & Straight Education Network (GLSEN) reports that one-third of LGBTQIA+ educators feel their jobs would be at risk if they were out to their administrators and one-half of LGBTQ+ educators feel their careers would be at risk if they were out to their students. More alarming, only 12 percent of LGBTQIA+ youth see school as an affirming space. All students, both Black and Queer, deserve to have committed classroom teachers who are reflective of their own identities and are teaching affirming curriculums. I knew it would not be easy carrying all of this. But stepping off the commencement stage, I had the utmost optimism in what could be accomplished. With the weight and the pressure I persisted.

Talking to my nana on the phone is a time I both look forward to and sometimes avoid. It's a family rule that you never go more than 72 hours without returning a phone call or she would track your location and show up in person. "Which one do you want?" she often said. I could not help but laugh not because it was funny but because I knew it was true.

The seventy-two-hour rule changed when I moved from Michigan to DC. Distance doesn't do anything but make grandmas worry twice as much. We went from talking once every three days to talking every morning on our way to work. She was on her way to the Ford Motor Company headquarters, while I managed DC traffic to my first teaching job.

I love my nana, Lord knows I do, but it is not always an easy conversation. She, like most Black grandmas, just have a way of extracting the truth from you and then reading you for absolute filth. And all in love. Here's a simple example. When I moved back home I was adamant about moving into downtown Detroit because I wanted a "city lifestyle." She rebutted with, "You should certainly check out the apartments around the block [from my mom's house] before you rush into making a decision."

Yeah, right. There were a lot of things I wanted to do and living close to home was not one of them. After only a few searches, I signed a lease for an apartment in the thick of the action. I enjoyed hearing the hustle, being in walking distance of the Detroit River, being close to my friends, seeing the skyline at night, having access to Whole Foods since I was newly vegan. Only two weeks into my stay did I realize that I really do value quiet. The vroom of the motorcyclists and the let-out from the outdoor amphitheatre around the corner was just too much.

> *Boy. What did I tell you?*
> *You're going to start listening to me one day.*
> *Take your time.*

My nana doesn't sugarcoat much. I should've taken my time. I should've looked at a variety of places. Her "I told you so" was coating every minute of that call. It was in that tough moment that I started to think about all of our daily phone calls, my mistakes, and what lessons I'd learned throughout my life. The throughline has always been slow and deep reflection should be my best friend.

Reflection is the most critical practice of an effective teacher. It's making meaning of your past in order to make change for the future. Too often in education, we are forced to make decisions without having enough time to truly reflect. We're juggling mandated curriculum, teacher evaluations, standardized tests, harmful disciplinary practices, pandemics. I repeat . . . pandemics . . . and all the complications that come with it—lack of access to Wi-Fi, limited access to devices, families dealing with financial and health crises, the huge learning curve of virtual learning and teaching. It can feel overwhelming to make reflection a part of your life as an educator but it's important to do so. Why?

Because we have been fighting an uphill battle, even before this pandemic.

According to the National Center for Education Statistics (2015), 8 percent of teachers leave the profession yearly and another 8 percent move to other schools, bringing the total annual turnover rate to 16 percent. More alarming is the fact that turnover rates are 50 percent higher for teachers in Title I schools and 70 percent higher for teachers in schools serving the largest concentrations of students of color (Learning Policy Institute 2017a, 2017b). Moreover, 80 percent of teachers are white and 77 percent of them are female. People of color make up about 20 percent of teachers and a mere 2 percent are Black men. And we know, specifically, that Black teachers make a difference. A Johns Hopkins

Patrick, Not Pat :)
@PresidentPat

[VULNERABLE THREAD]

This is my 6th year of teaching and I'll be teaching in my 6th school. Yeah, you read that correctly. Over the past several years, during the "first five" years of teaching I have really struggled to find a school community to call home.

I know this is not normal. It's not something they tell you to prepare for in undergrad. It's not ideal. Each year I stepped foot in a school building, I had every intent on staying for the long run because I planned to be a "career teacher." No one could tell me different.

Aug 13, 2020

economist found that "having at least one black teacher in third through fifth grades reduced a black student's probability of dropping out of school by 29 percent. For Black boys who live in low-income neighborhoods, the results are even greater—their chance of dropping out fell 39 percent" (John Hopkins University 2018). Without a doubt our impact is significant.

So, like my nana told me, "Take your time."

I started writing this book when everything in my life was normal. I was twenty-five years old living in Washington, DC, in an affordable apartment. I was finally out and proud. I was newly inducted into our country's first and greatest Black intercollegiate Greek fraternity. I was documenting my school year, week by week, on my *Common Sense* podcast, racking up thousands of listens and creating traction on my personal social media accounts. And all of this was intersected with working at my dream school, teaching dream content, working with Black boys. After working in three schools, in three years, it felt good to settle. To be normal. Meeting my incredible editor to craft a book about the experiences, latest research, and best practices for educating Black boys in our education system seemed like an exciting next step. You couldn't tell me nothing. Until I was fired in the middle of the year.

It's funny how these things happen. Everything that I knew to be true became murky. My confidence had depleted and the pain was mickle. Who was I? Did I belong in this profession? How do I maintain my credibility online? I knew nothing else but to vamoose. I packed up all of my bags and went overseas to start over in Qatar, where foreign was my new normal. Deep in depression, anxiety, and homesickness, I had nothing but time and space. Quiet and reflection. Normal can't exist without *no*. And so it was here that I had to get clear about what I truly wanted, what I really believed in, and where I was going. My amazing editor Holly told me to just embrace the journey.

I know I don't have to convince you that there is a lot going on in the world. I know I don't have to know you personally to know that you have a story of your own. I do not have to convince you of the dangers of our society pushing the world to do business as usual in the most uncertain times. Global conflict, sickness, systemic oppression prove how interconnected we are every day. Yet our society's answer to these issues is and has always been: individualism and normalcy. It is normal to attend countless education conferences, trainings, and online chats, and they all are hyper-focused on telling teachers what to do and ensuring that they know how to do it quickly. I too wanted the grab-and-go, tell me what I need to know, because the pressure was always on. Test scores have to increase yesterday. Pop-up observations could happen at any minute now. We are in the midst of a pandemic and the world is looking to teachers to clean up a mess we didn't spill.

I want this book to help you to release that pressure. Creating change in our education system and our greater society is a long-term game and I need you here: fired up, ready to go, and whole. This book will not tell you what to do. Instead, this book will ask you to reflect on what you have experienced. This book will just ask you to dream big about what you want to be true for yourself, personally and professionally, our students, and our education system today and tomorrow. I wrote this book with the belief that teachers are human beings doing human work every day. Thus, if we want to be the best at our jobs, we need to know more than just what to do. I strongly believe that teachers must begin sharing our stories, not just our strategies.

The First Five is a collection of short stories, timeless lessons, and big questions from my first five years as a classroom teacher. This book is a memoir but with a call to action. When this book is released, I will be in my seventh year of teaching in my sixth school. I have seen education through a plethora of schools: traditional public, traditional charter, tuition-based private, tuition-free private, international, homogeneous and diverse, wealthy and beneath the poverty line. I know what it means to move away from home and teach in another state; to board a plane and teach overseas; to be fired in the middle of the school year; to heavily consider changing careers; to win national education awards and be featured in national publications; to see students start the year as nonreaders and leave above grade level; to watch students grapple with social issues and develop action plans; to push against the system and fail; to be fired up and tired. I know from these experiences that we all have more in common than we do differences across disciplines and contexts. You better believe with all of this, in just seven years, I have a story to tell.

My experience teaching is anything but normal. So it is only right that this book takes a different approach. Each chapter begins with a story from one of my years of teaching. I want to immerse you in my world. For some of you these stories may be preachin' to the choir. Feel free to write *amen* in the margins. Some of these stories may be completely

REFLECTION IS THE MOST CRITICAL PRACTICE OF AN EFFECTIVE TEACHER. IT'S MAKING MEANING OF YOUR PAST IN ORDER TO MAKE CHANGE FOR THE FUTURE.

different than your teaching experience. This is *my* truth. The book is not chronological, but it includes stories across my first five years. And I will warn you now, within my truth is a range of emotions. Embrace the journey. I won't leave you hanging.

Within each chapter, you will also find an array of visuals. I am a teacher that still loves finding pictures in adult books. These visuals are meant to be used as paired texts. Some pictures are directly from my home photo album. There are some photos that are historical, literal, and abstract, helping me to help you understand the lesson each chapter illustrates. You may also find bits of poetry and quotes from a range of educators both traditional and nontraditional: teachers, philosophers, Ballroom House parents, students, authors, and more.

I like to label myself as a fantast. This means I am a dreamer. Each story leads to a lesson. These lessons work together to make me the educator I am today. Don't view them as isolated. Further, I often find myself asking big questions I don't have the answers to. Each chapter's lesson leads to a Big Question at the end. It is my hope that these questions will help spark long conversations with your squad. I hope that it will push you to affirm or change your own thinking and develop your own solutions. Big questions are the match that lights the spark. I have also learned that I must be more specific. In the spirit of my nana, I have included slow and deep reflection exercises that you can engage in individually, with a small group or PLC, or with a large group. These reflection exercises may require varying levels of vulnerability.

While the book is centered in my experiences, I know from tweeting and meeting educators from across the world that we all have stories. At the end of each chapter, you will find reflections from a diverse group of educators. These interviews were transcribed from Zoom interviews I conducted. There are teachers in their first five years, veteran teachers, international educators, former teachers, and administrators. We all have something to share.

I am an author who is still a current classroom teacher. Please know that I wrote this book to teachers and educators from a strength-based perspective. It means that I see you. I acknowledge the hours, the work, the blood, sweat, and tears you put into this profession. I see you. I acknowledge the trainings you have attended, the degrees you hold, and the expertise you possess. I see you. I acknowledge the amount of money you've spent and frustration you feel when you attempt to catapult change in our system. I see you. I acknowledge how overworked and underpaid you are in a system that has more than enough to provide you stability. I see you. I wrote this book as an educator for educators. I will never speak to you from a deficit.

It is also important to clarify that this book is very teacher centered. I believe that when teachers are seen as human beings, then students too will be benefiting academically, spiritually, emotionally, and intellectually. So yes, teachers, this book is for you. However, my biggest fear in writing this book is that those reading this book will believe that I am too teacher centered when this work is about students. I talked with my close friend and fellow author Lorena Germán, and she told me, "Teacher centered is your approach to writing but not your approach to practice." I love it when my friends get me. This book is for you, and this work cannot move without you, but we know we do it for the kids. You must know how important you are to this work. I recognize your humanity. I want to extend grace. I want to build community with you, teacher to teacher. And it is my hope that the work we do together will leave you empowered and ensure that you stay in the classroom for a few more years. And in turn you will empower your students and they will recognize the power of seeing the humanity within themselves. You are a model.

And so I guess this is the part where the introduction ends and the book begins. I'm a little nervous. Can you take a deep breath with me?

> **Get still.**
> **Recognize your breath.**
> **Take a slow inhale through your nose.**
> **Recognize how your chest puffs up.**
> **And wait.**
> **Then, slowly exhale through your mouth.**
> **Maybe you recognize the sounds around you.**
> **Or maybe you look around and notice something new.**

I am just one piece of a larger picture. But still, like you, my story matters. I have made mistakes. I have not done everything right. But through deep and meaningful reflection I continue to learn. And I am still here. I am so looking forward to your reflections, your critiques and affirmations. We are in this together, for the long haul. Here's to the next five years.

se w

re or

ject ti

instantl

eople.

ough

uld

h

ti

get the

ensure

this bas

o on the

sketba

Why are you always hang

n't do that

a kickball; you want to

wrestling; here s a

tball; hit a home run with

ys don't

Where are all of your

that current

ould not be

integrated

s not to say t

ools doesn't ma

the responsibility

that we have a safe

ents to process what

ening in our world

istory. That'

that

CHAPTER ONE

I LIED ABOUT MY WHY

 Patrick, Not Pat :)
@PresidentPat

Why am I going into Education?
Those kids at camp saved my life.
Being a Teacher is the least I can do.
(plus, it's fun and rewarding)

Apr 23, 2015

 Patrick, Not Pat :)
@PresidentPat

I originally got into teaching because
grading papers is soothing. But now, I
know the power of being a conscious,
reflective black male teacher teaching
black kids. Still Grading papers calms
all my nerves.

Dec 2, 2019

AT THE BEGINNING OF THE YEAR, WHEN THE EXCITEMENT IS STILL HIGH AND FLOORS
are still shiny from wax, administrators are eager to begin the year with a familiar
question: What is your why?

Sometimes, we are instructed to journal in notebooks or take an artistic approach
on chart paper to hang around the staff room. We are told that we must always
begin with our why because it is the secret energizer when Darktober arrives. Or
when you and your students are restless in the middle of a long stretch. We are
assured that beginning with your why sustains you in this profession that is often
difficult, ever changing, and thankless.

And every time I am asked to share my why, I tell a few half-truths. This is the story
I share.

The adults in my life loved me and poured into me in the best ways they knew how. Since birth, I have been around adults who are educators in their own right because they are storytellers. On the east side of Detroit, my aunts would blast Cameo and Earth, Wind & Fire and tell me about their first concerts, fusing in music history. My dad would show me endless legal pads of his own wrestling storylines, bridging his imagination with reality. I sat next to my grandmother exchanging commentary on our favorite soap operas. On family vacations heading down south, my grandparents did not just tell me how big the world is but showed me. I spent a lot of time eavesdropping. Or being in grown folks' business. Listening to what had happened while my mom was on the phone or grown-ups sat in the living room hashing out their current struggles. The adults around me kept me close. Sometimes with intention and sometimes without knowing, I learned how to actively listen and how to empathize. I learned about how proud I should be to be Black and from Detroit. I knew how to enact revenge (if necessary) and how to repair relationships. I learned how to create, sing, and dance even if someone was looking. The adults in my life were my first educators.

I spent a lot of my earliest years on the "North End" of Detroit. An industrial hood, cornered by train tracks and expressways. Not known for generational wealth but rich in community and culture. I can still smell the Father's Day neighborhood barbecues where we'd gather en masse. We did not need permission to gather daily at the community center and neighborhood playground. Everyone knew each other. My family stayed on Delmar Street. My great-grandmother Margaret lived in a green, two-story family duplex on Delmar Street. I would stay there during the summer and on weekends. My cousin lived across the street and my aunts two houses down. Everyone went to Loving Elementary School around the corner.

At four, I would walk alongside the important women in my life to Loving Elementary School to drop off and pick up my older cousins. When crowds of eager kids would spill out from the double doors, I looked forward to hugging Mrs. Wellet, my cousins' preschool teacher. She was tall, her skin was a chestnut brown, and her gray hairs flaunted her wisdom. She was the community's grandmother. Her classroom was bright, filled with toys, and larger-than-life play sets. She knew my mom, my grandmother, my great-grandmother and taught all of my cousins. And though I was not her student, she knew

William C. Loving is the former Vice President of the Detroit Federation of Teachers. He joined Detroit Public schools in 1935 and was the first Black male teacher assigned to an elementary school.

me. When the morning bell rang, the tears would flow. My parents remind me often, "You were always so upset because you wanted to stay."

My natural curiosity about what happened behind school walls and my "maturity" for my age did not go unnoticed. Folks would ask me what I wanted to be when I grew up, my parents had no problem interrupting them midsentence: "This boy is going to be a teacher." They didn't stop there. They completely invested in me. Santa Claus brought me a chalkboard and parent–teacher conference forms, way too many stickers, and teacher edition workbooks. I'd spend hours making sure my World Wrestling Federation action figures knew how to add and sound out words! And then hours grading their papers.

I'll never forget the day Mrs. Wellet asked if I could stay. In that one question alone, I knew she saw my potential from the inside out. This is the magic of school. There are symbols of togetherness in communities that can be felt at all ages. Even though I was one semester away from being eligible for preschool, I spent that day and many after soaking it all in. Crisscross applesauce on the circle for story time and cheffing it up in the play kitchen. I thrusted my fists in the air, I was king of the world on the playscape before flipping through all the books on the shelves and slipping into dreamland. The year it was my time to enroll in Mrs. Wellet's class, my joy spilled over. During the next two years, I would explore the world and possibility in a single room. This is the magic of teaching: making space for kids with unconditional love, community, and imagination. I wanted to be a teacher, too.

Sometimes I tell people that I wanted to be a teacher because I had phenomenal teachers in Southfield schools. Southfield is a suburban city, a next-door neighbor to Detroit. In its inception, Southfield was a predominately white and Jewish neighborhood. According to the Census Data (HUD Office of Policy Development and Research 2000), in the 1980s, Southfield was only 9 percent Black. My grandparents and my mom were part of tripling the percentage of Black Southfield residents to nearly 29 percent in the 1990s (Southfield is now nearly 80 percent Black). My grandparents wanted to move in 1992 (one year before I was born). The reasons for moving to Southfield varied for Black people in the 1980s and '90s. But for my grandparents who were working full-time at one of the big automotive companies in the city, Ford Motor Company, they just found a house they loved for a great price. "It was just a good

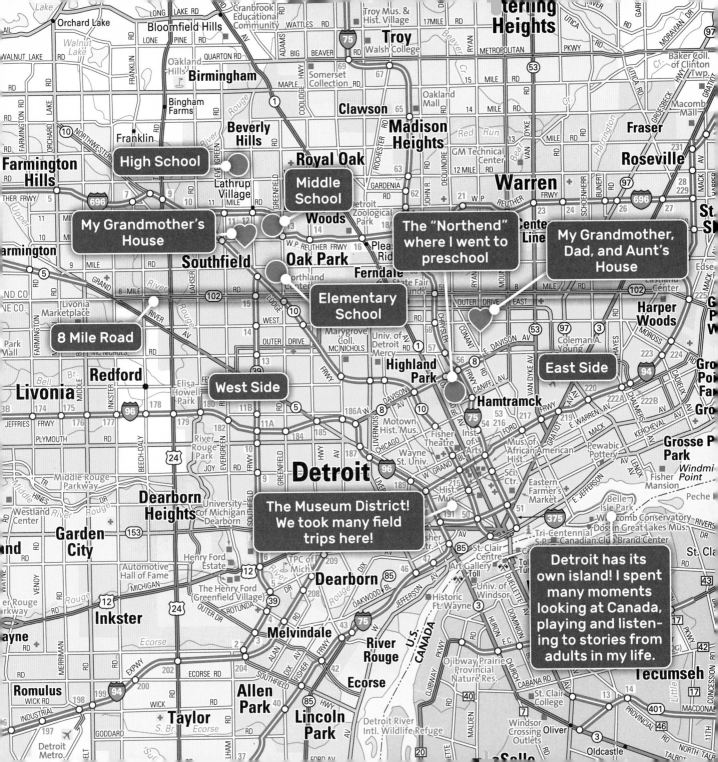

place to be. It was also one of the first suburbs that were welcoming to Black people who were on the come up."

Still, getting there would be no easy task.

My grandparents found their dream home two miles north of 8 Mile Road, the long stretch that separates the city of Detroit from the suburbs. A typical suburban home: two stories with four bedrooms. In a quiet neighborhood. Safe. Green grass, tall trees that created shapes on the concrete from the shade. And Black folks on the block. Their dream home was owned by a white couple and the selling process was managed by their realtor, a white man who lived next door. "The house was a great price at the time. We did everything we could to get the house," my grandparents reminded me.

Each bid they put in was denied, denied, denied. It was not until my nana met the owner outside her dream home that things changed. My nana tells me, despite being denied, they got along well. They got along so well in fact, the owner wanted my grandparents to have the home. She told them she thought they would take care of the home they had built from ground up. My nana looked at her puzzled. "But you denied our bid three times."

The woman looked at my nana puzzled. Even after checking with her husband, nothing. Not one of my grandparents' bids on their dream home was reported. My grandparents explained, the realtor next door, the gatekeeper and key holder, was holding the house for a white family. "They weren't even approved for the house yet. We were preapproved and had a down payment." Despite the realtor's grotesque games, the owners made the decision to accept my grandparents' first bid. And as my grandparents moved in, the realtor next door moved out. Deuces.

All of that was worth it to my grandparents and my mom because the icing on the cake was my being eligible to enroll in Southfield Public Schools in 1999. At the time, Southfield Public School district was a highly rated Black school district and sought out by many Black families within and outside of Southfield city limits. Like all schools, behind the veil of excellence stood a body of teachers who would teach more than what could be measured.

I had my first Black male teacher in fourth grade, Mr. Hobbs, now a county executive. He taught me the power of storytelling. My elementary music teacher, Mrs. Hodge, was a former Black chamber choir member. She introduced me to cultural traditions around the world and taught me to have confidence and pride. My middle school choir teacher, Mrs. Wynn, was a critically acclaimed gospel artist. She taught me to trust my voice, even when it was changing. My high school marketing teacher, Dr. Cook, was a Black woman and was the first person I called "doctor" outside of a medical office. She taught me the value of hard work and authentic leadership. My AP English teacher, Mrs. Maas, was an actress and voice-over artist. She taught me the power of words and dream chasing. These teachers and many more poured into me their expertise and creativity. Most of all, from the very first day they were authentically themselves. They made school, even in the midst of all the kid drama, a place that I looked forward to coming to every day. We exuded excellence because they were sheer excellence personified. My grade school experience showed me the art of teaching. While I cannot recall the AYP or the school test scores (the mere indicator of our public reputation), I do know building relationships with my teachers, the projects we completed, the units we explored, the clubs that pushed me, made the possibility of education as a career all the more congenial.

Many of my teachers in Southfield Public Schools were settled into their classrooms at least ten years by the time I stepped across the threshold. I watched my teachers go up against school boards face-to-face for fair contracts, strike for wage increases, and show up even after 9/11 attacks and the 2008 recession. I witnessed them adapting to change with the introduction of the No Child Left Behind Act. Still, they coached academic games and organized school plays. They made their college rivalries public fun. And my God they facilitated dynamic learning experiences. My teachers stayed put and fought on.

Their unwavering commitment to the profession and our community gave me big shoes to fill. But I was up for the challenge when I became the first in my family to leave Detroit, one of the Blackest cities in America, to travel seventy-five minutes west to attend college at Michigan State University where Black students were only 7 percent of the student body. The bulk of my time in the number one Elementary Education program in the country was spent on learning the science of teaching, designing lesson plans without boundaries, and investigating how systems of oppression impact teaching and our students. In my practicum, I was tasked with identifying ways students and teachers were disadvantaged due to school policies. I wrote hypothetical papers synthesizing my observations and developing theoretical solutions. These rigorous assignments helped me to clarify my values and think about what is possible for our students.

In addition to academics, I spent time doing what college students do, figuring out who I was and what I stood for.

While rigorous academics helped me to form my ideals the reality simply exposed dissonance. In the first few weeks of college, I stood shoulder to shoulder with my Black friends and our allies protesting in-your-face racist acts. Just a week after classes began, "No N*ggers Please" was posted on a Black student's door, only two rooms down from me. A Black doll was hung with a homemade noose in the Engineering building in the middle of the night. Though I had grown up in this Black neighborhood celebrating myself and my culture, I felt ill-equipped to emotionally grapple with the in-your-face racism. And so, I just experienced it and took it in. Racism was something I knew had happened and continued to happen before I got to college. But through my Detroit childhood, I had never seen it so up close.

These emotional moments allowed me to explore aspects of my identity that I did not get the opportunity to growing up. In college I learned that race was a social construction and not a biological reality. In college I learned that I was bilingual: I am a native speaker of African American vernacular English. I learned from Dr. Jeanne Gazel, of the Multiracial Unity Living Experience, what it means to be interconnected and how to facilitate conversations on race with my peers who had differing opinions. I marched for Trayvon and laid in the streets for Mike Brown. In college, I learned that being Black is not a monolith and that the experiences of

Black people are vast across the diaspora. In college, I had an unmovable love for being Black and still knew that I wanted to live in a society where we were all liberated from the shackles of oppression. I knew that after I walked across that stage, liberation was my mission. And I knew that teaching would be my contribution to the world for getting there.

I am a teacher because I had phenomenal educators from my living room to the classroom. My family invested in my love of teaching and education. My teachers in K–12 taught me that teaching is an art form. In college, I gained a sense of purpose. I tell people that I am a teacher because education is a pivotal key to continue unlocking liberation for marginalized groups, but particularly Black Queer people. Teaching in schools is my daily protest to systems of oppression. I know that I have always been destined to teach.

And that's the teaching origin story I tell. But it does not end there.

Please be advised: sensitive material

When I was eighteen years old, the summer before I went to college, I quit my job as a server assistant in a fancy Italian restaurant. My life would change forever when I received a call from a number with an area code that was unfamiliar to me. "Is this Patrick Harris? I'm an assistant camp director and I heard you're passionate about kids." A man with a deep voice and enthusiasm called to let me know that I had been recommended by someone in my high school to fill a vacant camp counselor position at a historically cost-free summer camp for youth who could not afford expensive summer programs.

I laughed at first. Because how did you get my number again? But also, I had gone *glamping* (glamorous camping) but had never been to a real summer camp. I mean skyscraper trees surrounding a beautiful lake where the sun's reflection rested comfortably. Cabins with only two outlets and the silence of city sounds. The camp was two and a half hours away from the city of Detroit, near the west coast of Michigan. This new experience was an opportunity for me to make money before college doing something that I loved. It gave me a chance to give space to my independence bursting at the seams. The answer was yes.

When I arrived at camp, I was met at the entrance by the assistant camp director. He was a Black man, over six feet tall, had a wide smile, and wore mismatched clothing. He shook my hand and hugged me like he had known me for years. I smiled and said I was glad to be there and away from my home for the first time. I had never been to Kalamazoo, Michigan. It was one of those cities that I knew existed, but never fathomed I would visit. In Michigan, unless you're headed to school, we usually stay in our place. I had no reason to travel to the west side of Michigan. I knew no one. But the welcome from him told me I was where I needed to be.

Growing up most people would say that I was a good kid. I was a part of the National Honor Society and other prestigious clubs in high school. I played piano and I did what my parents told me to do. Most importantly, I was going to college. So when the assistant camp director came to me within the first few days to tell me that he wanted to mentor me I immediately looked at him. My eyebrows went up, my lips twisted, and my face said, "What? I don't need a mentor." I had never had another Black man approach me in that way. To see me not as perfect Patrick but as a young, impressionable Black man who did indeed need guidance. Still, I told him no. "I need to get to know you more. I don't know what I've gotten myself into being at this camp. So let's get to know each other, let me feel out this camp and then maybe I'll let you mentor me." I had no idea what a mentor even was. I thought mentor programs were only for the "bad kids." For those with behavior or academic concerns. I was never sought out for mentorship programs in my community because I was a "good kid."

On the dock of the lake the evening before the kids arrived for the first day of camp, my assistant camp director shared his coming-of-age story. Hearing him share the deepest parts of himself, to know he wanted to share his struggles and fears with me gave me a sense of relief. Vulnerability is our greatest superpower. "Me too," I said to myself over and over. To hear and see the vulnerability of another Black man without the mask of masculinity left the door open for me to share. I talked about my fear of failing in college. I talked about feeling seen in my upbringing but not heard. I even revealed that I was curious about my journey with sexuality. I told him I might be gay, but I was unsure. Without hesitation, he looked up at me and put his hand on my shoulder and said, "This is why you would benefit from being my mentee." I joined the trees in laughter. I hugged him and I said, "Alright you can be my mentor."

Over the next several days our relationship grew stronger. He made sure all of my needs as a camp counselor were met: having enough materials and supplies, checking in on me to ensure that I felt seen and safe, calling me out to sing songs in front of the group. He gave me extra leadership roles. I was having the best time.

As campers cycled through the camp experience, the relationship between me and my mentor turned dark. While children were napping in the middle of the day, I was in the corner of the cabin where I had more privacy. I would wake from my nap to the assistant camp director, my mentor, next to me unannounced. Touching me in ways that made my heart beat fast. I couldn't scream because I was surrounded by children whisked away in a peaceful slumber. I couldn't run to the car because I was deep in the woods and there was nowhere to go. I couldn't drive home because I wouldn't be able to explain this to my parents. I couldn't tell anyone because my body said it was my fault. I must have done something that invited my mentor into my cabin bunk, not just once or twice or three times but over ten times.

And the question I get most is how did you physically make it through that moment in time? I tell people it is because after those dark moments I would escape the mental marathon by experiencing the relationships I built with my campers. Their laughter, their joy, the lightbulb moments that went off when they learned how to swim or they finally hit the bull's-eye during archery gave me the will to move forward. They saved my life. They loved me and accepted me for who I was even with my imperfections. They high-fived me and told me thank you when I needed to hear it most. Times when I didn't think life was worth living they were there for me without even knowing it. And so the other reason I teach, that I don't often tell people, is that I am paying back a debt that could never be repaid. It has brought me healing. Those kids at that summer camp, two hours away from home, saved my life, and now, I'm giving back to them in the form of education. And that's the full truth. That's why I'm here. That's why even during the most troubling times, I choose to stay and fight alongside and for my students.

So what's your story? You know, systems of oppression count on you to count yourself out. People in positions of power depend on your complicit silence. No longer. Tell your story. Whether you're new or seasoned. What really brings you to this work?

To be clear, it's not wrong that schools and districts ask teachers to reflect on their why in the beginning of the school year. It's good practice. But the ways in which we extract life stories from teachers in the beginning of the year, in my experience, has always felt cheap. In my time as a teacher, a lot of these activities were centered around motivating teachers during challenging times. "You must know your why, it will ensure you're motivated to keep going (aka staying late at school or grading papers on your weekends)." And we share it and it's done. Chile, bye! With a hyperfocus on labor, we lose the power of our own healing. We lose the understanding of how our stories help us to empathize and connect with our colleagues and most importantly, our students.

It can sometimes feel overwhelming to think about yourself in a profession that's "not about you." We cannot ignore investigating our why. It cannot be set aside or assumed. Because at the core of your why is your humanity. Understanding this helped me to rephrase a common statement that has defined my entire being: I am a teacher. When I sat in my why, my story, my pain, my trauma. When I processed it with myself, my therapist, my friends, my colleagues, I was able to come to the realization that . . . I am not a teacher. Instead, I am a human being that teaches. That's a crucial distinction. Putting my humanity first allows me to give myself grace when the system won't. When I recognize my humanness, it allows me to take mental health days without feeling guilty. When I recognize myself as human, I have greater empathy for my students. It allows me to reframe the work that I am actually doing. Teaching is not just about achievement or content. It's less about grading papers and writing lesson plans for likes. I stop worrying about how decorated my classroom is and working long unpaid hours after school. I am able to breathe. Why? Because I now see education and teaching as human work. And now, I can enter the profession whole. Focused. Ready. If we are ever going to be the teachers our students need, we have to reflect our humanity back to them. If we ever want to tear down systems and rebuild them in love and equity, we must see education and teaching as human work.

You will hear people in power say that this work is not about us. They will tell us to keep it about the kids. And we should, to a degree, understand that the decisions we make as professionals are about the development of young people. But when we don't see education as human work, we fail students by denying the humanity of their educators. We cannot fully recognize and honor the humanity of our students while silencing and devaluing teachers' stories. It's also here that we learn our beliefs, our biases, and our values.

Dr. Yolanda Sealey-Ruiz speaks about the importance of self in her work, pushing teachers to dig into their Archaeology of Self. In an effort to understand complex issues of race, sexuality, gender, and other intersectional identities, Dr. Sealey-Ruiz believes it is important for teachers to unpack their stories because it gives them a clearer understanding of how they show up to the communities they serve. She acknowledges that we, particularly those who are Black and Brown and Indigenous, are still healing from historical trauma. Embedded in this work is a deep, critical reflection of our "real" why. Without knowing who we are, where we come from, the pains we have faced, the traumas we have survived, we will not be able to truly show up in this human work for students or ourselves.

I am here because I am in love with teaching as an art form. I am here because it is a necessity; education is a key to liberation and joy for all. I am here because I know whole and happy children can heal the land with the support of loving and caring adults. I am a human being that teaches. I am human. And I am here.

And so what brings you to this profession? Not the professional version you tell your colleagues in an activity. I mean, your real, unedited story. From the beginning. The one that you know deep down in your heart pulled you into teaching. The story that brought you into the profession, despite every known challenge educators, students, and schools face daily. The story that keeps you here in the midst of it all. Let's start here, with you and your humanness.

Take a deep breath. In and out. Allow your air to walk through your nose and notice how your chest rises. Keep the breath there for three counts before you release it through your mouth. You might want to do that twice more. My story is heavy and maybe the story behind your why is too. We will uncover this together and discuss how it manifests through your teaching.

BIG QUESTION: How did your upbringing bring you into this work? How did it shape the educator you are today or the educator you want to be?

There are two ways you can tackle this work. If you're feeling inspired and ready to write or speak, you can answer the central question. Follow your gut and see where it takes you. If you want more of a guided experience, I've written some detailed questions below. You could answer a few them or all of them.

Our Selves

Let's start here. I'm asking you to dig deep here, to give yourself permission to be your most vulnerable self. If you have access to someone whom you trust, sit with them and take turns answering these questions. If you're with someone, what commonalities and differences do you hear? Explore these. If you are in a crowded area or with people whom you are just getting to know, start with journaling these questions.

This reflection might lead you to shuffling through family photos or scrolling through your camera roll. It might lead you to searching old tweets or calling a family member. Dig Deep.

> *What are your earliest memories of schooling?*
>
> *What messages did you receive about education growing up (i.e., from your parents, pop culture, advertisements, government)?*
>
> *How did your identity shape the ways you experienced education? (You might consider race, place, gender, sexual orientation, etc.)*
>
> *How do your earliest messages of school show up in your why and your teaching? Are these healthy for you and your students?*

Our Schools

Let's keep going! The next set of questions are going to ask you to think specifically about your schooling experiences in each level. These questions could go deep or stay on the surface. I will always push you to dig deep, particularly if you are in the company of colleagues who you will work with through the year or people you trust. Again, if you're with someone, what commonalities and differences do you hear? Explore these. The following questions require some level of vulnerability. Sharing and listening to a small group of colleagues will help you to learn more about your why.

> *What were your elementary, middle, and/or high school experiences like? Who were your teachers? How did they make you feel? What were the most memorable moments? Why? Were they mostly positive or negative?*
>
> *How did these experiences impact you as you embarked on your journey to become (or avoid) being an educator?*
>
> *How do these experiences and your evaluation of them show up in your why and your teaching? Are these healthy for you and your students?*

Our World

Let's extend outward on this one. The final set of questions can be answered on your own, in a small-group or in a large-group setting. They speak to a broader experience and may lead to commonalities. The questions are designed for you to share your experiences with a large setting, such as an entire department or your school faculty.

> *What world events took place during your K–12 experiences? How did these shape you as a young person? Did this influence how you thought about yourself in education?*
>
> *What does your government believe about education? How does this show up in policies? How does this impact how you show up?*
>
> *What do you have in common with your colleagues? What does this reveal about your why? What does this reveal about our education system?*
>
> *What fundamental differences do you have with your colleagues? What is the root of these differences?*

Whether you've finished or are just getting started, shout out to you for giving yourself permission to tell yourself the whole truth. This is a good time to write out a why statement. Be cautious of the ways you speak about your truth. Speak it with power, with your chin up. Let whatever emotions surface from your gut. Hold your why with you everywhere you go because it is the key to your humanity. I see you.

TEACHER REFLECTIONS

Holly S., New York
Seventh- to twelfth-grade English language arts teacher
Years in education: 15

Q: *How did your upbringing bring you into the work? How is it keeping you here?*

A: I went to a pre-K kind of school in the '80s. It was inside of a church basement. There were two teachers there. I'll never forget the day we had a school play based on a nursery rhyme. I had one line as the little dog who laughed. But when the time came, I had to be given a cue by my teacher. My teacher looked so angry because I fumbled my line. And she made me sit in a naughty chair and I had to face the wall. I'm saying to myself, I can't believe I'm sitting here.

My mother was so upset about this. She told my teacher, "You don't have to shame a child for feeling fear or uncertainty." My mom was my first teacher and a protestor. She did not go to a four-year college; she went to high school, some community college and that's it. She never had trouble speaking her mind. Both my mom and dad told me [education] was the most important thing that would help us move on from where we were.

They were working class, old school. They told me, "You don't need to bring home As and Bs. Give it your all and reach." My mom had this thing. She kept telling me, "Never stop learning." I took it literally because I never stop taking classes. I'm in school now.

My mom taught me the meaning of acceptance and pushed to stand for something. Being Italian and Sicilian, we had a wide variety of skin tones in our family. This brought up issues of colorism in our own family. Even in the midst of confusion or conflict, my mom and grandparents always made it a point to love us aloud. What an honor to be raised by such human beings. I want that [for my students].

I want them to have a space where they see themselves reflected. It keeps me up at night. I don't want them to feel the way I felt in the naughty chair. And I know it does not have to be a physical chair. It can be done with a look or a comment. Am I making a child feel like this? I need to pause, reflect, acknowledge it, apologize for it and make it right. I'm not sure if I do it as often as I need to. It's one of those things I think about a lot. I want to be an educator I'd like to have.

Jourdan B., New Orleans, Louisiana
Art educator
Years in education: 9

Q: *What are your earliest memories of schooling?*

A: The earliest memory of school brings me back to Ms. Tina, my godmother, who would babysit me as a child. I was maybe two or three. This was where I learned about family as a value, I learned what family should be. I learned about cultural norms: dances, what coffee was, video games.

Everything you would expect to do in a huge family, I did with Ms. Tina. Being with her reminds me of what education should feel like. She made it safe and created a really nurturing environment. When I would pee on myself as a child, no one ever teased me. Haha. You know instead they would take care of me. Family.

Q: *What did your parents tell you about education growing up? What messages about school and education did you see on your favorite television shows or in advertisements?*

A: My parents always told me that education was important. And that I needed to stay in school. But they also told me [education] was my own personal journey. For example, when I was in the third grade. My friends and I got really good grades on our report cards. At school I learned from my friends that we got things when we got good grades. We talked about things we would get (allowance, new games, clothes, etc.). I did not know what I was going to ask my mom for. The day came, I gave my mom my report card. She was happy for me. And I asked my mom, "So what do I get? Do I get a gift or allowance or something?" She looked me and she said, "You got those good grades because you worked for it. The prize are those great grades, not a reward from me or anybody else. When you get bad grades that's when I step in. But, if you're doing good, you should be proud of yourself. You should be accountable for your own education." Ever since then, I've always been the type of person to take ownership and accountability over anything I do. The reward is the education.

Q: *What world events took place during your K–12 experiences? How did these shape you as a young person? Did this influence how you thought about yourself in education?*

A: Y2K happened. There were the twin towers (9/11). I saw the first Black president get elected. But nothing compared to Hurricane Katrina. Being a native of New Orleans, you're always around Black kids. You are in a Black city. But when the hurricane came, we were evacuated to a city outside of Dallas to a place called Seagoville. This was the first time I had to interact with groups of white people and Latin people on a large scale. You could say it wàs "diverse." In New Orleans, I was in a sixth-grade class with twelve students. Then, I went to Texas where the seventh-grade class was 300. I had never been in a space that was that big. I was used to one class and one teacher. One lunch line and one lunch period for everybody. Everything is bigger in Texas.

Q: *So, how does your upbringing, all you've mentioned, bring you into this work? What does this mean for you as an educator?*

A: Even as a photographer and artist, all of what I have experienced pushed me into education and it allowed me to notice the injustices in education systems. I have seen the ways money determines what type of education you receive. I have worked in wealthy private schools and alternative schools. Children are the same but institutions are not. For example, when I was working at school where the tuition was 5k a year, they did not get detention when behavior was a concern. Instead, they did yoga and meditation. And they have procedures in place that help them to navigate their emotions. But public and charter schools I was in felt completely opposite. All too often, I heard "One more time and you're going to jail." I knew that every child needed a chance.

Art allows for personal development, identity, and expression and helps you explore who you are. In my class, we are allowed to be dreamers. We use art to bring our dreams to life, we imagine our superheroes. We create visions for our future. It feels like a therapy session in an unconventional way. We have stories. And all of these experiences contribute to the ways I show up with my kids.

CHAPTER TWO

TEACHING IN 360 DEGREES

Patrick, Not Pat :)
@PresidentPat

My advisor told me because I'll be a young, black, male teacher. I can write my own ticket to any school in the country lol #collegelies

Nov 20, 2011

IN FOURTH GRADE (2002), I HAD MY FIRST BLACK MALE TEACHER. HE STOOD OVER SIX feet tall, was of average build, and wore wire-framed glasses. He wore clothes that made me and my friends snicker. "They look like girl clothes," some of my friends whispered. He had a mean finger wag and a piercing snap that you never wanted tilted your way. He did not act in the same manner that the gym teacher or the other fourth-grade teacher did, the only other two Black men in our building. Looking back, my teacher had mannerisms that were not hypermasculine. We labeled him as different. It's why we laughed. It's why we made jokes. He was the rose that grew from concrete. Beautiful, yet unusual, questioned and scrutinized.

When I got home, I would tell my parents just how "different" my teacher was. "He acts like a girl." I would imitate his snap and finger wags (I would never share how much I enjoyed that). His difference led my mother to, in a way that only she could, politely ask

BOYS (1993)

SIT UP STRAIGHT

WALK WITH ONE FOOT IN FRONT OF THE OTHER

DON'T YOU DARE CROSS YOUR LEGS;

BOYS DON'T DO THAT

WE'RE WATCHING WRESTLING; HERE'S A BASKETBALL;

CATCH THIS FOOTBALL; HIT A HOME RUN WITH THIS BASEBALL;

HOW ABOUT A KICKBALL; YOU WANT TO GO ON THE SWINGS;

BOYS DON'T DO THAT

WHY ARE YOU ALWAYS HANGING WITH THE GIRLS;

WHERE ARE ALL OF YOUR MALE FRIENDS?

BOYS DON'T DO THAT

ARE YOU WEARING A TIE OR A BUTTON-UP FOR CHURCH? BLACK OR WHITE?

YOU ACT LIKE A GIRL;

BOYS DON'T DO THAT;

WHY DO YOU TALK LIKE THAT?

LIP SMACKING AND PROPER. PRONOUNCING EVERY SYLLABLE.

BOYS DON'T DO THAT.

WHERE'S THE SWAG IN YOUR WALK? ALL I SEE IS SWITCH.

DON'T STAND LIKE THAT. UNCROSS YOUR FEET.

BOYS DON'T DO THAT

WHY IS YOUR WRIST LIMP? STRAIGHTEN IT.

BOYS DON'T DO THAT.

DON'T CRY.

OR I'LL GIVE YOU SOMETHING TO CRY ABOUT.

AWW. HE'S SENSITIVE. BUT BOYS AREN'T LIKE THAT

HE CAN'T FIGHT. HE WON'T FIGHT. LOOK AT HIM STANDING THERE;

BOYS DON'T DO THAT.

CAN I ASK YOU A QUESTION?

DO YOU HAVE SOMETHING TO TELL US, PATRICK?

DON'T WORRY I WON'T JUDGE YOU.

DON'T WORRY.

YOU CAN TELL ME.

(written in my 2021 Queer studies class, inspired by Jamaica Kincaid's poem, "Girl") to see the principal after she dropped me off at school. Before breakfast was over, I would be cleaning out my desk and transferring it to the classroom next door. My new teacher stood just a few inches above five feet. He was a Black man, wore shirts and ties daily, was part of a Divine Nine fraternity, and was obviously more masculine. He was a typical rose—admired, predictable, unquestioned, and seen.

At ten years old, I internalized that boys being feminine was iniquitous. And it could lead to consequences. Those two continents don't meet. The way a boy walked, the way he chewed or told stories could leave him alienated or worse: targeted. Before I knew what it meant to be queer, I knew what it meant to be different. I snickered at my own teacher to keep my friends' eyes off me. If I laughed hard enough at my own teacher I could make my inherent femininity invisible. Deep inside, I knew I was a rose in the concrete too. I just had not blossomed yet.

Growing up, I hated the way I walked. Whether I was walking with my friends from the cafeteria to recess, or from my cousin's front porch to the community center up the street, or taking a few steps from the couch to the kitchen, I was always calculating each step. One step in front of the other, with a slight lean for swag. My hips needed to remain straight, they could not sway in the wind or move left to right. My hands needed to remain in my pocket, balled up in a fist depending on where I was walking or who I was passing by. I had to be careful not to let my wrist bend at 90 degrees. Whenever I reached my destination, my growing feet needed to be facing forward, not one straight and the other backwards revealing a natural fifth position. Walking for the approval of others was a mathematical equation I could never solve.

One of the best parts of transitioning to middle school was knowing that my nana's house was within walking distance. For once, I was no longer a bus kid. Instead, I was a walker. There was a certain coolness that went along with that title. Being a walker meant I was able to get out of school first. And my ultimate goal was to make it past the first stop sign before the school buses pulled off. I was rarely successful. Right behind me were three yellow buses. Middle school boys, some of them my friends, were usually hanging out of the window letting their pent-up energy from the school day unravel in ways only middle school boys knew how. "Patrick, are you gay?" Someone yelled out of the window. I looked up. "He is! He is gay!" Some other boy yelled to confirm. There was not a day that went by that some boy (or girl) in my school did not yell homophobic slurs and statements toward me while I walked home.

It was no coincidence that I put a first-generation iPod on my Christmas list my sixth-grade year. While they never failed to stick their head out of the window, even in the dead of winter, at least they were muted. I could not hear them over Queen Latifah's "U.N.I.T.Y.," or Cameo's "Word Up" or Jill Scott's "Golden." That first-generation iPod was the first time I exercised my own agency and silenced those who wanted to silence me. I felt unstoppable.

Whether it was the adults in my life or the kids at school, everyone wanted me to be who they thought I should be. A performance. I needed to be a version of myself that would give them peace and comfort at the sacrifice of truth. They wanted me to behave how they believed boys were supposed to act because of their own fears and their backdoor deals with misogyny and homophobia. I learned to adapt for my own safety. But their words and demands stayed near.

I have lost count the number of times I received kudos from my family, friends, and colleagues on entering the classroom as a Black male teacher. "We need more of you." "You are the unicorn of the teaching profession." They are not injudicious. Studies have consistently shown that only 2 percent of the nation's teachers are male educators of color. These data sit next to a Johns Hopkins study that show that students who have a Black teacher are 18 percent more likely to go to college. It sits across studies that show that Black male students who have a Black male teacher are 30 percent less likely to drop out of school. Effective Black male teachers increase the educational value of all students, but especially Black students. And educators know this. I have been involved in professional developments and nonprofit organizations that are geared towards developing and retaining Black male educators in the classroom. In 2018, I traveled to join the Black Male Educators Convening conference. I sat amongst hundreds of Black male teachers and allies assembled in historic Philadelphia to have necessary conversations about the state of Black male educators and our students. The keynote speakers were prominent Black men: Dr. Marc Lamont Hill, Dr. Chris Emdin, John King Jr., and others.

As powerful as this Black male educator's conference was, it would still not prepare me for the times I would be called queer slurs by my students. It wouldn't prepare me for the gut punch when I heard "that's so gay" and felt too fearful to say anything. It wouldn't prepare me for overhearing my sexuality being the topic of conversation

THIS WORLD IS FOR ME TOO,

HONEY.

THEY HAVE TO
UNDERSTAND THAT.

I HAVE A
RIGHT

TO BE HERE LIKE
EVERYBODY ELSE.

— OCTAVIA ST. LAURENT

in parent groups. And it certainly would not prepare me for the first time my first-grade class went off script.

I was the teacher to nineteen incredible first graders in my second year of teaching. This day was like every other day. We fist-bumped one another on our way into the room. We sat in a circle and listened to the morning announcements. I was even able to fit in an extra read-aloud before we began our phonics lesson. The calm settled, making room for chaos to ensue.

Literacy centers were usually an even mix between anarchy and organization. I sat at the infamous U-shaped table with a guided reading group, overseeing clusters of six-year-olds navigating their way through sharing and picture books and friendship and makeshift literacy games. While small fires sparked around the room, the computer station was always a source of peace. But this day was different. As we prepared to transition, the class paused at the sound of rumbling chairs and outlets. Two students at the computer station had gotten into an under-the-table kicking match. This was an easy fix. I hit them with the "Who started it?" *Rookie move.* One by one, students pointed to one student. Embarrassment and guilt made way for them to melt into a rage. Just before the chairs were about to topple over and the papers would fly, I looked at them and asked, "Did you?" *Really bad move.* Before I could just table this conflict, they screamed, "No!" And then, "Shut up!!" And then, "F*g!!!" It happened so quickly. The class gasped and looked to me. All I could muster up were two words, "Excuse me?" This was the first time in my life I had been called a homophobic slur. "He is. Because my mama said he is." They doubled-down on it with sharp articulation. My chest filled with air until an exhale was my only option. Then, incomplete breaths in rapid rates. Swelling eyes. Triggered.

No Black male teacher conference or statistic could prepare for this moment because the education system affirms me shining a light on being a man and uplifts my Blackness while pushing my queerness into the shadows. When I reflect on this moment, I think about how intentional I was about not wanting to put my gay on display.

Afar, I am a Black male educator, but I invite you folks to come a little closer. See all of me, my queerness too. I know I'm not alone. According to a 2020 Gallup report, the number of adults who self-identify as LGBTQIA+ has risen to almost 6 percent. The biggest contributor to this increase is Gen Z. One in six Gen Zers identify as queer. The closer we look at the report, it shows that the younger the generation, the more people self-identify as queer. To be clear, there are not magically more queer people, but we can infer that younger generations feel more confident in self-identifying as LGBTQIA+. You want to know a secret (even though it's not really a secret)? There are queer students in your school. Whether we make the choice to shed light on them or see them as a shadow demographic, they are here. When I began to identify as openly queer in my classroom, I opened the door for queer students to see me and my classroom as a safe space.

During the first full pandemic school year, I started pitching high-interest elective options for our students. In response to the Gallup poll and students coming out in our school, I pitched a Middle School Queer Studies and Literature elective to my department. I simply developed a syllabus that included course goals, required readings, assessments, and topics of study.

The main goals of the class were to establish a safe space for queer students and allies, to find community and engage in academic discussions around queer history. To my surprise ten students (this is a significant amount for my school) signed up for the course. It showed me that queer students were indeed looking for a space. In the beginning of the course, we cocreated norms and a set agenda to ensure the space was safe and to give us all room to lead. We began each class with students sharing songs that made them feel free and brought them joy; we opened the floor for a mental health check-in and group problem-solving; we read and dissected a piece of history or literature. We shared reflections and connections on a shared Padlet. At the end of the course, we created a virtual museum to share our biggest takeaways.

Our classes were filled with laughter from the gut, a wild amount of sarcasm, and many "Why are we just learning about this?" moments.

We traveled back in time to discover that indigenous communities have and continue to acknowledge those who fall between the gender binary. Two-spirit Native Americans embody masculinity and femininity and express multiple genders; third-gender or Māhū Hawaiians are highly respected; and hijras are legally recognized as a third gender in South Asia and are sought out for prayer.

We didn't stop there. Many of my students were fascinated with earlier time periods. So, we traveled to the 1700s and learned about queer resistance through Public Universal Friend and Deborah Sampson, gender-bending queer icons who directly opposed the constraints of religion. We spent time in the 1960s, talking about intersectionality with my personal hero, Bayard Rustin. "We learn about civil rights every year. We have learned about Martin Luther King every year since freaking preschool. But we have never heard of Bayard Rustin until now. I'm so angry about that," one of my students said. My students' curiosity in New York City as a place for Queer liberation led us to uncover the importance of Ballroom Houses and how they create endless possibilities for queer youth. (For more information, see *Butch Queens Up in Pumps* by Morton M. Bailey [2013] and Grinnell College's [n.d.] "Underground Ball Culture"). When I asked my students what their final takeaways from the class were, one of them said, "History is so gay."

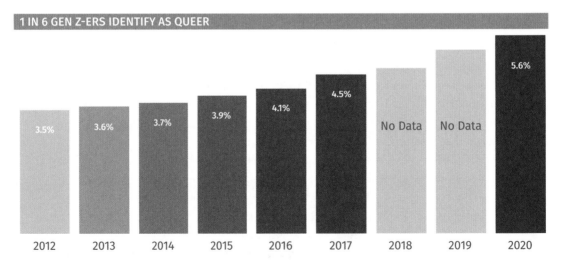

1 IN 6 GEN Z-ERS IDENTIFY AS QUEER

Gallup shows Americans' self-identification as LGBT (2012-2017 wording) rises to 5.6% in latest estimate.

One of the most memorable and timely units was about the state of mental health for queer youth. The COVID-19 pandemic was not equal in the ways it impacted the mental health of our youths. Towards the end of the course, the Trevor Project (2021) released a national report sharing 42 percent of LGBTQIA+ youth and more than 50 percent of trans and nonbinary youth seriously considered suicide in 2020. More than half of all nonbinary and trans youth seriously considered suicide. When you look closer, the number of Native American/Indigenous and Black queer youth was nearly double the number of white queer youth who seriously considered suicide. My students were empathetic. We dug into the research surrounding the grave concern of queer youth's mental health and developed arguments around our school's strategic plan to support queer students.

I looked forward to teaching this class because I could feel young Patrick sitting in the back of the classroom. He was no longer worried about his walk. He was not worried about what the boys would say when the bus passed him. Instead, he felt empowered and inspired. He felt fearless because he saw himself in Bayard Rustin. He was heard and affirmed when he saw himself in Willie Ninja. He felt healing and love when my students shared their own journeys battling patriarchy and overall mental health. This was the class young Patrick needed and he got it.

During the pandemic school year, my school's Gay Straight Alliance (GSA) was inactive, so there was no formal space, neither academic nor social, for queer kids and allies to come together to discuss the issues that were most important to them. This class filled that void. The relationships we formed through this class led to the revival of our school's GSA, which is now called SAGE (Sexuality and Gender Equality). My students would share that we found our chosen family. This was *their* house. I was their house father and they were my children. Our classroom filled a needed space for my students.

And the class continues. By the time this book is released, I will be teaching Middle School Queer Studies again with a new group of students—queer, questioning, and allies. I might have students take it again to dive deeper and colead and coteach. By the time this book is released, I would have released a series of queer coming-of-age stories on my podcast, *The Common Sense Podcast*. The work that we have started with this class will have an impact on my kids, my school, and the culture for years to come. This is human work.

"I don't in any way disparage any time I've had in the trenches because it really has made me the artist I am today." Billy Porter shared this thought after snagging a Tony Award for his starring role in the musical *Kinky Boots*. Throughout his career, Billy Porter gives us a masterclass in being authentically yourself and allowing who you are, where you've come from to show up in your art. He allows us to ponder the question: Can we do human work as anybody but ourselves?

Human work in education looks like this. Every day you walk into the school building, you're looking behind you. You want to be the teacher you wished you had, your friends needed, or replicate a really good teacher. You walk into the classroom every

day determined to be different. When you're scanning the room, acknowledging all of your students, you see yourself in the back of the room—the innocence in your eyes, your crossed feet, ready to go and learn. Each decision you make seeks to affirm that young kid in your heart. You're looking to provide healing to this kid and affirm them in the education system. You're pulling texts and designing lessons that would have the kid version of yourself jumping for joy. You make decisions every day for you.

At the same time, every day you walk into the building you're looking directly across from you. Maybe a dozen kids or two are looking right back at you. While you look backwards, you have to see the human beings you're teaching right now. You're listening to their stories, their wants and needs. You're building relationships with them. You are in tune with what makes them dance, what brings smiles across their face, and what brings out their passion. You recognize how technology is impacting them. You are making comparisons between your kid self and your current students; you might even be making judgments. Do not do this. Just listen and see your students for who they are. You are making decisions every day for the students in front of you.

As you're looking behind you and looking in front of you, you are also attempting to look far ahead. We know as educators this work is bigger than us, than right now. We want the content we expose our kids to, the skills they grapple with, the conversations they engage with to make an impact in their communities and on the education system. As teachers, every day we are making decisions to build a legacy. A legacy that makes change in your schools. A legacy that ensures the next class of students that walks through those doors of your school or educational place do not have to face the same systemic struggles your current students face or that you face. I see you planning ahead and speaking out. You want to build a system that ensures the teachers and students coming after you are in a system they won't have to heal from. You're inspiring your kids. You're tweeting your thoughts. You're attending school board meetings. You're on Clubhouse and Instagram live critiquing the system and sharing your story. You're dreaming big even when the system wants to place your thoughts in a box.

WE ARE LIVING IN **REVOLUTIONARY** TIMES.

— JAMES BALDWIN

Consistently teaching to the past, the present, and the future in concert can be overstimulating yet can echo the most beautiful sounds. This is our human work.

I was unaware of my role as the conductor when I began teaching queer studies in my middle school. I did not know at the time I created this queer course that it was human work. In the moment, I was just responding to the needs of my queer students. I did not realize the impact it had on me until I felt it in my gut each time the class met. And so, I wonder, how do we intentionally teach in 360 degrees?

It starts with building and sustaining relationships. As human beings, we thrive on positive connection. The very heartbeat of school is the thriving relationship between stakeholders. It also means that you are not ignoring your own story. Your own needs. It means acknowledging the importance of therapy and nurturing at least one relationship with a colleague in the building and having a strong support system outside of school. It means developing relationships with families and community members and understanding their needs; they represent the now and the future. Having relationships means being in tune with your needs, your students' needs, your families' and communities' needs, and understanding the trends of what's next.

I know you are already doing this work. I find more often that we're considering the needs of our students but still feel depleted afterwards. Have you considered the needs you may have in common with your students? In some cases, we're trying so hard to be the teachers we needed when we were young that we forget the needs of our students in front of us. There is room to fulfill all of our needs. With vulnerability and creativity, we have the ability to see the fruition of 360-degree human work.

Alright, alright. I know. You caught me being dreamy again. I know it's not that easy. I recognize that I worked at a school that aligned with my progressive values and trusted me with autonomy. This has not always been the case and may not be your reality; the process of acknowledging and then responding to the real human needs of yourself, your students, and what and who are to come can be in direct conflict with immense external pressures. I know it is difficult because we are dizzily dancing each day attempting to make magic and then boom: standardized testing; and then an unannounced observation; and pow: a COVID exposure in your building. But it's especially in these moments that your human work is most important. It's in the times when our education system intentionally goes against our human needs when our internal alarm clock should go off. What are we doing here? What can we do?

First, it's about acknowledging that teaching is synonymous with daily decision making. Every day we walk into school we are tasked with making choices. You know what this means? Autonomy. You have the power to make decisions for you, for your students, and for your legacy every single day. Nothing can strip that power away from you. It may help to determine where you want to start in human work. Is it best to begin intentionally planning for tomorrow or reflecting on yesterday? No matter where you start, know that this work is long term and it's a process. Give yourself grace. I see the work you're doing. I see the effort you're putting in.

Listen, as long as teaching is human work, it will require you to look back at yourself. So long as we are working with young people, we will have to meet their needs directly. And for as long as teaching is a human service, then we are invested in creating long-term solutions for our society. This is our legacy. We have always and will continue to do this work. It all matters.

So how will you tackle teaching as human work? What would be most helpful for you? Reflection or intentional planning? The questions that follow are the same but the framing of them can be in past tense to analyze a particular action you took in education. Or it can be future tense to prepare you to see the humanity in yourself and your students.

> YOU'VE GOT TO KEEP ASSERTING THE COMPLEXITY AND THE ORIGINALITY OF LIFE, AND THE MULTIPLICITY OF IT, AND THE FACETS OF IT. THIS IS NO TIME FOR ANYTHING ELSE THAN THE BEST THAT YOU'VE GOT.
> — TONI MORRISON

BIG QUESTION: How do our experiences and identities influence the ways we create in our classrooms and our schools?

The following questions can be answered individually or with a small group. The questions require some level of honesty and vulnerability. These questions can be answered in any order.

Go Back in Time

What teacher did you or someone you love need growing up? How would they have treated you? What would they have taught?

What's Happening Now?

Who do you teach? Who do they need you to be? Do you have the capacity, skills, knowledge, and tools?

What's Your Legacy?

If you retired today, what would your legacy be? How is your school, your community different after having you as a teacher?

What Now?

What do your answers have in common? What actions will you take? Do they satisfy all three questions equally?

TEACHER REFLECTIONS

Emmanuel Fisher
Former teacher and alternative education specialist, Washington, DC
Years in education: 27

Q: *What teacher did you need growing up? How would they have treated you? What would they have taught?*

A: I wish I had somebody more understanding. I went to Catholic schools at first. It was the 1970s and 1980s. My school was very strict. I still got paddled and got in trouble because I wrote with my left hand. I wish I had a teacher that would let me be a lefty and I wish I had someone who understood me as artistic.

I wish they saw my uniqueness. They told me I had trouble with comprehension. I used descriptors with the Dick and Jane books. If they asked me I would say, "Dick had on his Nike sneakers. Jane ran out in her yellow jacket to go over to the park." I added extra details instead of just sticking to the book. And my teacher took that as he can't comprehend it.

When I got to high school I had one teacher, he taught social studies. He actually inspired me to major in social studies. He was always in tune with me. When we studied medieval culture, he allowed me to do projects. He let me illustrate the meaning of the chapter and create images instead of answer true-or-false questions. He made social studies come alive.

Kevin O., Detroit, Michigan
Middle school math teacher
Years in the classroom: 9

Q: *What teacher did you need growing up? How would they have treated you? What would they have taught?*

A: I always talk about my education as being successful because of the supplementing my parents did: Black history, how race intersects in our current events, identity work. I didn't get it full blast in the classroom but I got it at home. I think I strive to be the socially conscious teacher that so many did not have when they were in school. I feel many of the youth in our city still don't have a full sense of how deep the systematic oppression runs and what they can do to fight against it.

Q: *If you retired today, what would your legacy be? How is your school, your community different after having you as a teacher?*

A: I believe I have been able to share a different perspective with students. As for every student I have taught, I was their first white male teacher who was born, raised, and lives in the community in which their school stands. I have been able to use my familiarity with our home as a way to make math more real by using field experience; we drove to the local grocery store, to see a math lesson come to life. I have also worked to introduce my students to parts of our region in which they may not have been as familiar. We took kids skiing for the first time and started a softball league. Embedded in all my legacy is my fiery level of advocacy.

CHAPTER THREE

FINDING A HOME

Patrick, Not Pat :)
@PresidentPat

\# Answering my calling today.
#firstdayofschool

⚙ Aug 25, 2015

I DID NOT CHOOSE MY FIRST SCHOOL, IT CHOSE ME.

After graduating from Michigan State's elementary education program, I panicked. My degree was conferred but $20,000 of loans and returning home to student teach unpaid stood between me and a certification. I joined Teach for America instead; this was the most affordable pathway for me to join the profession. This was *my* career.

As our cohort settled in our new home, Teach for America's DC region wanted us to know about a very strict policy called "the first offer." The policy was clear: you could interview with as many schools as you could earn. However, you must accept the first school that offers you a contract. Sort of like divine intervention. The school should not matter because the work is the work. Are you about educational equity or are you not? We were needed to serve students who needed teachers and leaders yesterday. My stomach tightened and my eyebrows raised. But I was here now. I wouldn't let my racing heart slow me down from reaching the finish line: becoming a teacher. I did not care what school I was placed in as long as it was public and I was in front of Black students.

Only a few days after I submitted my resume into the pool, I had a phone interview with an award-winning charter school. Twenty-four hours later they sent over my first offer. The school and TFA's sense of urgency left me out of breath. Before I could truly listen to my gut, I was signing the paperwork to join their new elementary school, only in its third year of operation.

And I'm not gonna sit here and lie to you. I drunk all of the Kool-Aid during summer PD. The energy transported me back to summer camp . . . almost. We were singing songs and clapping to call-and-responses. Teachers were passionate and enthusiastic; our leadership team was welcoming and encouraging. All of the feelings a new teacher needed to breathe.

We carried the momentum into curriculum design and first-day prep. We were paired with coteachers in every classroom. Together our task was simple: create a packet for each student, for each subject, for each day. Practice classroom procedures for every physical action you wanted students to perform, from the raising of their hands to the locking of their fingers in SLANT. (SLANT is an acronym used in schools across the country to control students' bodies. It stands for Sit Up, Listen, Ask Questions, Nod, and Track the Speaker.) This was teaching. Although packets covered the radiator and my clothes were laid out, the night-before-school jitters took over me. On my first day of school, I was optimistic.

You already know what happens next. I walked into my first classroom.

Innocent wide eyes.

Good intentions.

Fragile confidence.

And fresh packets.

Every plan corkscrewed. Lying between the extremes of my students' needs and my school's strict expectations about procedures, I stood in shock, voiceless.

My classroom was theme park chaotic:

lots of screaming,

running,

and tears.

I stayed after school until 6 p.m. preparing for the next day, just to fail. It chipped away at my ego and confidence bit by bit. And when I would finally get a moment to myself, I questioned if I truly belonged in this profession. My school's response was in-house and external professional development on giving explicit directions and consequences. They wanted us to focus on teaching like champions. Use explicit directions, hold students accountable, and smile. Not even their "support" could save me from my deep sink or swim mentality. And because I had flown hundreds of miles away from Detroit to make my dream come true and to make my family proud, I knew I could not drown.

Patrick, Not Pat :)
@PresidentPat

I pray that I never lose the night before Christmas feeling for the first day of school in my teaching career.

Aug 7, 2016

Autonomy for teachers was put under lock and key. And the only way I could access it was if I found a way to break the rules. I did what I've always heard from my own teachers—close the door and do what I thought was best for my children. It was time for a new beginning. We started by tearing up our packets page by page in celebration, recycling them, and picking up books instead. On another day, we flipped our desks over and turned our class into a spy lab to learn informational writing. My coteacher and I opened the floor to have open-ended class discussions about the issues our eight-year-olds cared about: homelessness, gun violence, why the world needs more Black wrestlers. After months of queasiness, we were at ease. And I wish that I could say the story ends there.

Our classroom was one piece of a large puzzle. Our school's leadership felt our entire school needed a cultural reset. The problem? Leadership concluded students across the school were not following directions because teachers were not clear in giving directions. Their solution? They wanted to pilot a new, nationally recognized program that coached teachers in the moment to deal with "off-culture" behaviors. They hired a consulting company that would come in to facilitate this innovative coaching strategy.

During my only planning period of the day, I received a knock at my door. My administrators wasted no time. "Patrick, we see how positive your classroom culture is. We know you would be a perfect candidate to pilot this program." I told you I'm not gonna lie to you . . . I drunk the Kool-Aid again. I was flattered that even as a first-year teacher, I was invited to pilot a program that would help move our school forward. I

Patrick, Not Pat :)
@PresidentPat

Sometimes I get random notes
like this in the middle of the day.
#Freedom

June 1, 2016

also wanted to gain the trust of my administrators so that I could make more change in the school. It felt like a win-win. And here's how the pilot went:

"This is a football game in the middle of the play-offs and you are the quarterback," they said. Prior to kickoff, I would meet with the administrators and the consultant to share my lesson plan. Then they set up my not so subtle "in-ear" headset connected to a walkie-talkie. "Listen close. We are your extra set of eyes. We'll give you feedback as you teach." This was the innovation. It was like a coach giving directions to the quarterback in the middle of a game. After they walked me through the directions, I took some time to think and adjust my headset. Then, it was time for kickoff. Coming in from recess, my students were already hyper and on ten because there were so many adults in the back of the room creating a cloud of whispers. The adults thought they would be invisible but my students saw them as aliens in our community: foreign, strange, and up to something. Just as teachers get comfortable, systems want to play a new game.

When the lesson began, I addressed the elephant in the room—my earpiece. I told my students the football story and they bought into it. "That's cool, Mr. Harris." They trusted me. After, it was time to give a very specific set of directions as a part of the pilot program. I had to tell students how to move, what their voice level should be like, and how to participate in a single sentence. And so I began, "Take out your pencil with your voice off, write your name on your paper, and begin the question. And feet on the floor."

Most students complied. As I was giving out thumbs-ups like Halloween candy, I heard a small whisper in my ear that said to give Sean a reminder. Sean looked like he was daydreaming so I reminded him that he should grab his pencil. They fizzled into my ear almost instantly.

"No." I was startled. With each piece of feedback, I froze. I could not focus on talking and listening at the same time. "Give him a consequence on the color chart so there is a visual consequence for everyone." Sean paused and his scrunched eyebrows stunned me. He blurted out "Really?" Annoyed, he grabbed his pencil, wrote his name on his paper, and began his work. Then I heard another whisper in my ear. "Praise students for getting out their pencils and writing their names." I complied.

It was typical for Sean to engage in very small, developmentally appropriate behaviors in the middle of a lesson that might distract adults who wanted control. He might get out of his seat and wander around. He might even try and talk to other students. He might even put his head down. If he was upset, we all knew it. But we created a space for him to be his eight-year-old self. My students and I have learned to work with Sean, not call him out publicly. But on this day, I had to see Sean under a microscope.

This day, Sean was a little slow getting back on task. He wasn't disruptive; he just did not comply with the directions at the speed the consultant wanted. I was instructed again to give Sean a consequence for having his feet on his chair when I said to put his feet on the floor. This was Sean's third offense or reminder, and I had to get on the walkie-talkie to call for support so Sean could "reset."

I was nearly in tears. Still to this day, I do not remember what the lesson was about. But I do remember taking a deep breath and telling my students how sorry I was for any trauma I may have caused them. I told them I would never put the earpiece on again. And I meant it.

In the debrief session with my administrators and the consultant, I fell apart. My students and I worked so hard to create our community. And in a matter of minutes it felt like a prison. My eight-year-olds were inmates forced to follow my direct orders with no autonomy or else they would then be whisked away. Their response was that if I truly cared about Black students, I would prioritize the skill of following directions. "If they don't listen to you and do what you say at the moment, what will that mean for them when a police officer pulls them over or another authority figure that has control over whether

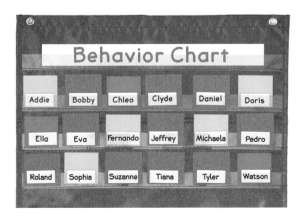

THE PRIZE AND THE **PUNISHMENT ARE INCENTIVES TOWARDS UNNATURAL OR** FORCED EFFORT, AND, THEREFORE WE CERTAINLY **CANNOT SPEAK OF THE** NATURAL DEVELOPMENT **OF THE CHILD** IN CONNECTION WITH THEM. — MARIA MONTESSORI

they live or die makes a request of them? What will happen to them?" Were we ushers in the school to prison pipeline?

That night I went home and reflected on my own elementary school experience. I thought back to a culture of undeniable fun. I thought about the times I was talking too much in class and how my teachers held me accountable with just a stare. Reminders made me cry when I was younger because I was a young perfectionist, but I knew that my teachers cared about me. I never associated my experience in elementary school with that of harshness or pettiness from the adults who signed on to care for me and love me. I couldn't sign on to do this program any longer. And so, I sent an email respectfully resigning from the pilot program. What happened next said a lot.

The next morning, I walked into school and everything seemed normal. I was on time for the daily morning huddle, I had breakfast with my colleagues, I checked in students' homework as they walked in one by one. As soon as I was about to begin a lesson, I was called to the main office. My leadership team wanted to let me know what they thought of my email. "We chose you because you were a star. We knew that you were ready and capable to lead this work. *This* email. It shows that you are being ungrateful, Mr. Harris." Ungrateful?

"My students cried after that lesson. I cried after that lesson, too. No. I just, I can't. I'm sorry." My words were jumbled. I wanted to communicate how it made my students feel and that their feedback was enough to sign off from this program. I wish I had said more at the time but I didn't have the language or confidence to combat the destructive nature of that program. My students' tears of resistance were left unnoticed.

"We want the same thing. We want students to be engaged, excited about learning. We want them to follow directions so they can get the most out of the amazing lessons you've planned. But also, you know the real-life consequences if "our" kids don't follow instructions. Imagine if the police pulls them over. I think you need to finish the pilot."

I hated how jumbled I came across. My confidence was too slippery to grab on to. I had no choice but to continue the pilot in my class or risk being fired in the middle of the year (at-will policies are no joke). After that meeting, I knew that the program would indeed live on without me. I felt intimidated, but I was able to articulate one last sentence: "We want the same thing, but we have two different ways of getting there. Our values are just different."

Those were my last words before I began looking for employment elsewhere.

Though I knew it was the right thing to do, leaving my school was not easy. I did not want to be a part of those statistics, like the one from the Learning Policy Institute (2017a) that states that the education profession sees a 16 percent turnover rate each year: 8 percent leave the profession, and 8 percent go to other schools. And that six in ten new hires in schools are replacing teachers prior to retirement. Education has a revolving door moving at warp speed. And I knew what my leaving would do to a school in Southeast DC. Turnover is not cheap. Districts in urban areas pay the highest cost, roughly spending up to $20,000 to invest in a new hire and not seeing the full benefit of the training and investment.

Teaching has always been my dream, so I just kept asking myself why. Why did I *have* to leave? Because that school was in direct conflict with my own values. We were not in alignment and they were not budging. Even if I chose to tough it out, I would not be able to do my best work there. I would not have an impact on students and

WHEN CHILDREN ATTEND **SCHOOLS THAT PLACE A GREATER VALUE** ON DISCIPLINE AND SECURITY THAN ON **KNOWLEDGE** AND INTELLECTUAL DEVELOPMENT, THEY ARE ATTENDING PREP SCHOOLS **FOR PRISON.** — ANGELA DAVIS

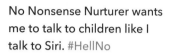

Patrick, Not Pat :)
@PresidentPat

No Nonsense Nurturer wants me to talk to children like I talk to Siri. #HellNo

June 12, 2016

that feeling of inner disappointment would ripple. I knew it would lead me not only to leave my school but abandon my profession. I was not willing to risk this.

Why was my school married to these values or ways of education? Knowing the history of a school can help provide a clearer picture of who they are and what they believe. My school was founded as part of an urban education reform organization. With the spotlight on inner cities, big money was awarded to passionate individuals with big visions and determination that exceeded their teaching and educational leadership experience. The visionaries visited high-performing charter schools, planned together, and were assisted with fundraising and support to start their schools in urban cities. The biggest catch was that the reform organization's core value was achievement and growth through test scores and numerical data. So it was not by accident that my school valued practices that pushed for a mechanical education. It is in their DNA.

Here are a few truths.

If we want to truly make a change in education, we need a school to call home. This means we have to kick our feet up and stay a while. This also means that we should be intentional about what homes we enter. When I was younger and asked if I could go over my friend's house, my mom went through a vetting process. "Who all gon' be there? Will their parents be home?" Then, to my embarrassment, she would ask to talk to my friend's mom. "I need to know what they about before I let my firstborn son over there!" I understood. My mother loved me and wanted to know that wherever I was going would not have drastically different values than the ones we had in our own house. She was intentional.

As teachers we too should feel empowered to be intentional. First, this means we need to look inward. We must always hold our whys close to us. Understanding our why and where we come from helps us to develop our own set of values. During my first five years of teaching, I did not think about my own values until I knew that they were being violated. All teachers, regardless of the number of years in the profession, should know what they value. I now know that I deeply value autonomy. I deeply value schools with decentralized leadership. I deeply value schools committed to equity and justice.

Then, you must search, find, and vet schools. This is where we determine if a school is right for you, if it is a place where you have room to make change long term and grow along the way. I will never tell you what to look for in a school. This is *your* decision. Every institution is different: varying histories, flaws, opportunities, strengths.

Believe me when I say, there is a school out there for you. In order to find it, we must do our homework. I will say it again. Do not settle for a home in which your values are directly violated.

This work is especially important for new teachers. As a new teacher, I was often told that I just needed to sit back and learn for the first five years, no matter where I was. Most times when we talk about the needs of new teachers, we think about them from a deficit mindset. But new teachers have value. They walk in the door with strengths and experiences. Teachers within their first five years should especially be picky in choosing their institution as it will shape how long they stay in the classroom and the profession overall. We are like sponges in our first years and incredibly sensitive. Our first schools play a large role in shaping the educator we become. As new teachers, we have to choose our schools wisely. There's no perfect school. Every school has its flaws. But what we have to determine in these first five years is whether the institutional issues at your school are in direct conflict with your values as a teacher. And if so, do you have the room, the group, the capacity to create change?

When teachers make a long-term commitment to their schools, it allows them to grow as professionals. Students are more likely to have greater academic and social gains. And communities and families are guaranteed to benefit. It's not just better for you; it's better for your students and it's better for the community you serve. We owe it to ourselves, our children, and our communities to find a school to call home.

> BUT SCHOOL SHOULDN'T BE PREPARATION FOR LIFE. **FOR YOUNG PEOPLE, IT IS LIFE.** YOUNG PEOPLE IN AMERICA WILL SPEND WELL OVER A FULL DECADE OF **THEIR LIVES IN SCHOOL,** BY LAW. THEIR DAILY LIFE IN SCHOOL IS THEIR **SOCIAL AND** PROFESSIONAL WORLD. IT ISN'T JUST PREPARATION **FOR IT. THEY DEMAND TO MATTER IN THAT WORLD, EVERY DAY.**
> — CARLA SHALABY

BIG QUESTION: Why is it important to see school as a home in this work? How can you make sure you're at home?

Before you move on to the reflection, you can take three approaches. You could answer these questions from the perspective of identifying your dream school. This is a helpful first step because it allows you to have a clear understanding of what you're looking for. You can answer the following questions and use a scale to determine if a school you're actively considering is a good fit for you. Or you can assess your current school to determine if you should stay or leave.

Your Why

Let's start with you. Reconnect with your why. What teacher did you need as a child? What school did you need?

What brings you to this work?

What are three truths or values you hold tight for your work in education?

Who Are They?

What is the history of your school? When was it founded and why? What is the history of the land it sits on?

What is the mission and vision of the school?

Do they have a list of values for their students?

Are They Who They Say They Are?

How do students describe the school? Who are their favorite teachers? What have been some of their favorite memories?

What is a typical day for a student? How does this reflect the mission and vision?

Where has your school allocated funds over the course of the last few years?

Do You Know Your School Community?

How many teachers are on your team? How long have they been there? How do they describe the school? What frustrates them? How do they work to solve problems in the school?

What does autonomy and teacher leadership look like in your school?

Who are your administrators or your leaders? How long have they been there? How do they describe the school? What frustrates them? How do they work to solve problems?

When your school makes a mistake, how do they address it?

Asking questions does not stop when you are hired. Being in conversation with yourself throughout the school year, particularly your first year, can help you decide if the school is home.

You and Your Home

How have you been welcomed into the space? What has orientation, onboarding, mentoring been like?

Where has your school allocated funds over the course of the year?

What does connection feel like? To your school? To your students?

Do you share similar values with your colleagues? Who's willing to join the fight towards a more just and equitable world with you?

Evaluation

How does it feel when you're in the building?

Are you able to be your full authentic self?

Are all of your identities honored and accepted?

TEACHER REFLECTIONS

Heather L., Seattle, Washington
Kindergarten teacher
Years in the classroom: 15

Q: *Let's start with you. Reconnect with your why. What teacher did you need as a child? What school did you need? What brings you to this work?*

A: I've had to really examine my why the last eight years. I've been in a school where I am a white teacher teaching kids of the global majority. I've had to evaluate my why through the lens of a savior. I've wanted to be a teacher since I was a little kid. And I was here to turn the world around. There's an excitement I get from a light bulb moment and the friendships they make. In kindergarten it's amazing how they play and grow and develop. They have so many ideas in their heads and teachers can squash a lot of those things. They're too young for this or they're too young for that. I continue to question why I am doing this and who am I doing it for. For me, it's about being there to push them further and let them think and affirm the ideas they have as little people. Their ideas are big. And outside the box. Long-winded answer to say I want to be able to help kids so they feel affirmed.

Q: *Why is it important to see school as a home in this work?*

A: I think teaching can be so personal. It is not just a job where you follow the protocol. There is so much wrapped up in how you teach. If it is not home, it is not going to feel right. It is going to feel like a constant push. When you think of family, there is always space to push because it is family. If you don't have that in a building there's a disconnect.

Ben W., Michigan
High school English teacher
Years in the classroom: 7

Q: *What is the mission and vision of the school?*

A: Together, teaching with excellence. It's a community mindset everyone is in this together, a place where professionals are valued, respected, and given meaningful PD.

Q: *Do they have a list of values for their students?*

A: Working Together, Excellence, Inspiring Students for Life.

Q: *What is the history of your school? What land does the school sit on? What is the history of the land? Of the community?*

A: I teach in a small city in Michigan. The board just voted to remove the CHIEF mascot. We have had several conversations with Indigenous people about how our school sits on their land.

Q: *What is a typical schedule (day) for a student? How does this reflect the mission and vision?*

A: A typical day would be math, science, social studies, English. One class each. There are usually electives. Students will double up in the sciences to make room for AP courses later in their high school career. There's a high focus on AP and colleges. There's also a growing population of students who are in a lot of remedial classes. There's an unspoken tracking system. Remedial classes cover the basics of reading, writing, speaking. The classes are primarily filled with ELLs/refugees/ students of color. Then, there's the AP track.

Q: *Has your school ever made a mistake? When your school makes a mistake, how do they address it and recover?*

A: I would say with mistakes, we are working to fix them. The whole changing of the mascot has been helpful. The school brought in a native leader and had an open Q&A forum with discussion and public comment. They were able to share their grievances. There have been types of town halls, where race + equity issues were talked about. You can see the concern on the superintendent's face. "Wow, we really messed up" face. The district has a well-thought-out response to address mistakes.

Q: *Are you able to be your full authentic self? Are all of your identities honored and accepted?*

A: Ninety percent yes. As a cis-white male, straight male. I am able to be myself 100 percent in that regard. I don't have to hide anything, change anything really. One thing that I do think about is my journey with cancer. I have not felt comfortable enough to share this with the community. It's just personal given the stigma of what it means to be a cancer survivor. I have shared it with some students who needed someone to identify with. I wanted to let them know that there is someone there with them.

Final Reflection

I am in a school that has some strengths but room for improvement. I feel empowered to make that change. This exercise definitely makes you think about you and yourself and how you fit. I was looking up information. You have to make sure it works. You want to be happy in your paying job. Your happiness and your willingness to put in energy, it's important.

CHAPTER FOUR

THE A-WORD

Patrick, Not Pat :)
@PresidentPat

How can teachers be artist if we're always using someone else's resources in our classroom

Patrick, Not Pat :)
@PresidentPat

I'm not saying don't share resources. It is important that we sit down and talk. But I'm just having a question about how we select resources, digest them, make them our own and then create something else.

Dec 29, 2018

IN HIGH SCHOOL, I WAS TOLD BY ONE OF MY TEACHERS THAT I SHOULD NOT PURSUE teaching. She taught one of many electives in the computer lab. Our class would sit in rows with bulging desktop computers staring back at us. During one of our conversations, she sighed and said, "They think they can replace us with computers. They will try. Who knows if they're even going to need teachers in thirty years?" She cackled all the way to her desk. This idea of teachers as robots was something we joked about throughout my high school years and something we talked about more seriously in college. Could computers actually replace teachers?

Replacing teachers with computers is not a new discussion. Let's go back in time, shall we? In the early 1800s, there was a man named John Lancaster who immigrated from London to the United States. He was a teacher and an education reformer. When he arrived, public debates were erupting around supporting schools in low-income areas: large class sizes and unruly behavior were amongst the biggest concerns. Hiring trained teachers was expensive and school districts could not afford it. But John Lancaster had an idea. Instead of making one teacher responsible for educating large class sizes and to answer the call of order and discipline in the classroom, he developed the monitorial system.

The monitorial system trained and paid students (all boys), also called monitors, to teach students in small groups when class sizes were large. Large bodies of students, ranging from 200 to 1,000 pupils, congregated in large lecture halls. John Lancaster taught the monitors the lessons and the monitors taught the students. Lancaster utilized the latest technology: the optical telegram. It would show visual codes to alert the monitors. For example, *M* would alert students to show their slates or an *S* would alert monitors to meet Lancaster at the front of the room for a team huddle. The classroom was indeed robotic. The method caught the attention of

white missionaries running American Indian schools. They needed assistance educating who they claimed to be "unruly" children. While Lancaster's #edtech innovation was deemed influential by many educators in power, others pushed back and complained their children were losing instruction by trained professionals. We are still in the 1800s.

Education is like the update that pops up in the corner of our computer. Several times a day it asks, "Would you like to update your computer?" If you're like me, you say, "Not now." Over and over again, "Not now." Despite the reformers and the outcries, education today still looks and feels like Lancaster times. The COVID-19 pandemic forced our society to look in the mirror to see, yet again, the answer to an outdated argument: you cannot replace professionally trained teachers with technology or any other one-size-fits-all curriculum.

Schooling can be standardized but education cannot. As long as we see education as human work, then teachers must have and exercise their autonomy.

> **Autonomy (*n*): A state of independence and self-determination in an individual, a group, or a society. The experience of acting from choice, rather than feeling pressured to act.**

Imagine second grader Angel learning mathematics. Eight years old. In a freshly ironed uniform, face shiny from Vaseline. To the average teacher, they are well behaved. They sit with their hands folded, eyes straight, feet on the ground. But when math comes, they are eager. They try hard to raise their hand, but they just can't help but to blurt out the answer. Finally, they can let their confidence shine. But their teacher gives them reminders to give someone else a turn. They wait, tapping their foot and humming now. The child looks behind them and sees the assistant principal in the back. The assistant teacher is walking around helping those who are stuck. As the teacher explains the concept, going through each step thoroughly, Angel is growing more and more agitated. They have already completed the "I do" portion before the teacher finishes. They raise their hand, but their teacher gives them a look. Angel decides to draw now, profusely, on the page. Planets, stars, shapes each with their own distinction. Their packet is nearly black. Stars have exploded with pencil dust. When the teacher walks around to check on students, the only thing visible on their packet are answers and the stop sign in the bottom right corner. They ask, "Can I move on now?"

In my first year of teaching, I taught second grade in a school that had an unhealthy marriage to the gradual release model. I do. We do. You do. That's it. It was the only pedagogical practice modeled in our professional development and measured in observations. "This is what the research says works" and "If we all do it correctly, then all students would learn" they would often defend in our professional development sessions. We were praised for flipping the model when it was time. You do. We do. I check. All of our student-facing instructional materials were teacher-made packets of warm-ups, fill-in-the-blank notes, and practice questions. Students were explicitly taught to pay attention to the stop sign in the corner just in case they wanted to go ahead. Our school held tight to a coteaching model: each classroom had one lead teacher and one associate teacher. I was the associate teacher in my second-grade classroom. My lead teacher, a white man from Virginia, stood at the front of the board while second graders took notes. And I was the "monitor" walking around ensuring students were keeping up. We were not allowed to stray away from the packets or the gradual release model in the name of equity. All students received the same materials, the same instruction, and the same approach for each subject, every day. As gatekeepers of knowledge, we were in the way of students' learning.

My students were hungry for knowledge. They made their own plates, filled their own cups. And just when they satisfied their curiosity and were ready for more, I snatched the cup from them, poured it out, and made them watch the nourishment lay across the floor. And the funny part is that I knew exactly what my students needed. I was not clueless. I was ignorant of how to create change and felt powerless. Early in my teaching career the weight of what I was "supposed" to do collapsed onto my students, leaving us both suffocating.

Chris Emdin (2021) recognizes teachers as professionals in positions of power. He pushes us to challenge systems of power for students' achievement. "Students must see you struggle with the tension between what is expected of you and what is the right thing to do" (2). I knew the right thing to do. But the weight of the curriculum, the lack of support, the pressure from administrators, unknown observations, my own perfectionism, made choice look like a myth. I had no choice but to do what I was told or else. Or else I'd be fired or I'd be told if I didn't follow the curriculum I'd fail. Within Dr. Emdin's simple push is the belief that all teachers need autonomy. And what we do with that autonomy, those choices, makes us liberators or oppressors.

In the early summer of 2017 things changed. I accepted a position in a private elementary school (progressives now call them independent schools) as a fifth- and sixth-grade English and social studies teacher. This was my first time working in a private school.

One of my school's missions was to provide an alternative schooling option to families who did not have access to the high-cost, ivy-adjacent private schools that were tucked in the richest parts of Washington, DC, Maryland, and Virginia. *Those* schools. My school was different. First, students did not pay tens of thousands of dollars to attend. Our school was tuition free. Second, it was a single gender school that served nearly 100 percent Black and Brown boys from kindergarten to sixth grade.

And the last major difference: we were not housed in a traditional school building. We were inside a renovated apartment building in a working-class community in Northeast DC. We were not tucked away; we were part of the community our students came from. My school was unique in the sense that we were fully funded to be fantasts: to create a school for Black and Brown boys to be themselves and to have an opportunity to find their passions without pressure from oppressive educational systems.

This was my third school. By this point I knew what to expect. I wanted to get whatever curricular materials ahead of time so I could start planning early. But Mr. Williams had other plans. I sat across from him and he took a deep sigh and smiled saying, "Look, Mr. Harris, there is no curriculum. This is why you are going to be so great in this role. We're going to rebuild the academic program for these boys. I have a boxed curriculum here to help with a scope and sequence. But we won't use it for content at all. Here's a list of unit topics I covered last year." He handed me a laminated, color-coded paper that had a table full of unit topics and themes: from Black inventors to the Tulsa race riots to the transatlantic slave trade to the Civil War. His smile read, "Are you down for this?" I answered the call. Now this is the challenge I had been waiting for after graduating from my teacher education program.

Before my boys could tackle any of those heavy, vast topics on my principal's chart, I took time to get to know them and to work with them to establish our community. We spent six weeks reading and writing stories on perseverance. We worked together to determine community guidelines and talked about the need for restorative community meetings. We went outside for lunch, listened to music, shared poetry, did a ton of independent reading together. When conflict arose in our classroom, we solved it as a class in community meetings (which sometimes took longer than expected). I learned about their passion for eradicating homelessness in our nation's capitol, their frustrations with the lack of reparations, the abundance of racism, and just how legendary mumbo sauce is. And so when our master bedroom became too crowded or our Wi-Fi went out, we had a culture of laughter and love to fall back on. While we were busy building community, I was using my autonomy to go into deep study.

Our first unit was "What Is Race?" It was an interdisciplinary unit that allowed students to seek evidence and draw conclusions on the origins of race and racism. Before I could teach this unit, I had to do my own work. I spent my lunch breaks and evenings deep into the writings of Eric Foner and Howard Zinn. I was neck-deep in Toni Morrison's interviews and essays, as I wanted to ensure I avoided teaching through the lens of the *white gaze*. I watched PBS' *Race: Power of an Illusion* (Adelman 2003). Having this level of autonomy made collaboration a natural next step. Having my essential questions and final assessment reviewed by my colleagues or my principal no longer felt like judgment day, but just another perspective on the art I was creating. I scheduled the bus to the National Museum of African American History and Culture. The only step I missed in all of this was seeking my students' feedback as I was designing their learning experience.

The eight weeks we spent deep-diving into the origins of race allowed my boys to develop a critical lens. We started by learning about the earliest humans, observing their skin tone and their origination in Africa. We read primary sources of racial scientists, and with their science teacher, the students learned about DNA ladders. Together they discovered how race was a social construction but racism was still real. We learned from PBS how racism and slavery predate race. We went to the National Museum of African American History and Culture to connect with the plight of our ancestors. They interviewed their parents and caretakers on their attitudes towards race. We shared our most impactful artifacts from our field trips. We learned how to pen an informative essay and wrestled with the idea of explaining race. By the end, my students had a strong vocabulary and understandings of the beginnings of race. Most of all, they had a lens to look through. They were eager to connect their key takeaways with the future units we covered. While there were hiccups along the way, I grew as an educator and as a Black man because the autonomy that came with this teaching position gave me time and space to learn.

My friends, let's be clear. This is not to say that teachers should not follow their school's curriculums or pedagogical suggestions. Talented educators and curriculum writers earn degrees, use research, and work collaboratively to build comprehensive curriculums for students across the world. Further, we know that there are also teacher entrepreneurs who also are talented curriculum writers in their own right. However, there are many teacherpreneurs and curriculum companies that sell their products to teachers and institutions in the name of higher test scores, increasing engagement, being culturally responsive, and "saving time" (and capitalism). Some of these products are valid and useful. This should lead us to question online educational marketplaces. There are online sellers who are providing an alternative to curriculum houses, but research shows that, within this large volume of teacher-made materials, quality and copyright infringement is an ongoing issue. And more so, their content model equates classroom holiday decor to curriculum

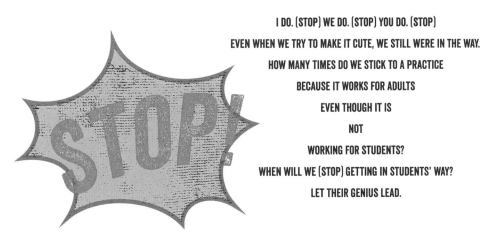

I DO. (STOP) WE DO. (STOP) YOU DO. (STOP)

EVEN WHEN WE TRY TO MAKE IT CUTE, WE STILL WERE IN THE WAY.

HOW MANY TIMES DO WE STICK TO A PRACTICE

BECAUSE IT WORKS FOR ADULTS

EVEN THOUGH IT IS

NOT

WORKING FOR STUDENTS?

WHEN WILL WE (STOP) GETTING IN STUDENTS' WAY?

LET THEIR GENIUS LEAD.

as if they are equal factors to what defines an education. But as professionals, we know that we cannot simply copy a lesson plan, a unit plan, or a textbook script. We owe our students more. This strips away the power from our students before they get a chance to step up to the plate. Instead, we must know our students. And we must know ourselves.

Teachers need autonomy to respond to the nuances in front of us. Our children are complex human beings growing rapidly and exposed to more media than ever before. People of the global majority are exposed to racism before they even have the opportunity to understand it. Students are facing trauma at alarming rates. Curriculum won't solve this, but autonomy will.

In 2015, during Teach for America's twenty-fifth anniversary, I was completely fed up by my school's grip on what I could and could not do. If you should know anything about me, it is that I am never afraid to challenge a panelist at a conference. During a session on teacher autonomy, the CEO of the New Teacher Project was advocating for new teachers to have scripted lesson plans while they "learn how to teach." I rose to the mic to ask them when they believed new teachers should be given autonomy. They boldly said: "After their fifth year." Autonomy is all about power. And with the power in the hands of corporations, curriculums, CEOs, and not in the hands of students and teachers, it allows for inequity to continue. I laughed and stated, as a first-year teacher, that taking away a teacher's autonomy creates a barrier between teachers and students, it does not allow for teachers to develop their own instructional identity, and it rushes them through the revolving door. Over the years, I have learned that there are four types of autonomy.

Autonomy is complex. We must ask ourselves what autonomy means to us. Our schools and districts may have different definitions than we do. We want to be on the same page about the ways we design learning experiences for and with our students. Autonomy may vary school to school and state to state depending on a myriad of factors. Education is a high-stakes, heavy-pressure profession. To fall into compliance with higher powers or to achieve a score on a test, there are districts who feel less inclined to give teachers autonomy. Administrators may be hesitant because they made a late hire. Teachers may find it not worth it to challenge authority for more autonomy out of fear of losing their jobs. It's best to start with understanding what type of

When your institutions have full control over what and how you teach and interact with your students.

NO AUTONOMY

This type of autonomy happens in part or whole. It may look like being forced to use a basal, or a pre-made script, using a lesson plan or unit plan template that is non-negotiable.

When you take your autonomy without notice or permission.

TAKEN AUTONOMY

This happens usually in response to feeling trapped. You know you must act or your students will be negatively impacted. This can feel empowering when your autonomous decision works. A cloud may come over your head if your decision does not work the first time.

When you perform well and your administrator allows you to experiment in your classroom.

PARTIAL AUTONOMY

Ultimately the control of students' learning is in the hands of administrators or team leads who may or may not be inside the classroom. This can make teachers feel replaceable. With strong relationships and healthy collaboration, this could help new teachers ease into their autonomy so they don't feel overwhelmed.

When autonomy is a part of your job. You have the ability to have full control to make decisions on behalf of your professional journey and your students' learning.

FREE AUTONOMY

It puts the power in your hands to make instructional choices so you can share it with your students. For new teachers, it can feel overwhelming if you are new to the profession without training. But, it does leave ample room for authentic collaboration.

autonomy *you* need. I've learned that I am my best when I have *free autonomy*. I need the least amount of restrictions, with content and skill scope and sequence, as possible in order to fully grapple with the learning targets, to exercise my creativity, and to be able to fully respond to the needs of students. Too many boxes leave me feeling trapped and create more work for me. I know there are teachers who do not share this sentiment. Depending on a teacher's level of comfort and expertise, they might say that they want less autonomy and more direct support from their colleagues and administrators. This could help to strengthen their expertise on a certain pedagogical skill or give them more time to study a theory. Sometimes too much choice without enough support can feel daunting. Throughout the year, teachers and administrators should feel empowered to discuss autonomy and support openly.

What are you willing to risk to empower your students?

The ultimate benefit of teacher autonomy is knowing that the power of choice can be directly shared with our students. If adults have autonomy but students do not, then we have a problem. To be the best teachers we can be, we need autonomy. Autonomy allows us to craft experiences directly for the students that are in front of us. It allows us to directly respond to the needs of our communities. My brother José Vilson (2020) says, "Students won't ever trust you with their minds if they can't also trust you with their persons. Building relationships is part and parcel of equity work."

Autonomy unleashes the imagination. Schools and districts must find ways to get out of the way of students' and teachers' success. Instead of making all students learn the same content in the same way or silencing teachers' instructional voice, schools and districts should ensure teachers and students have the right to make teaching and learning personalized for them. There should be an ample amount of time for teachers to collaborate and plan with one another. Students should be surveyed frequently, allowed to choose what content they engage in and how they show their learning.

The work is too big to be fit into a box.

At its core, autonomy is not just about choice, it's about power. How will you use it to be the teacher your students need?

I have a strong belief in your professional judgment. Now comes the time for reflection. Let's explore the autonomy you currently have or are seeking from your school.

This is best done with colleagues you trust. It can also be done alone or in a large group with a facilitator. It's best to start off defining autonomy in your own words. (You can use the definition I gave you!) This helps you to have a foundation. Then I'm going to ask you to think about the autonomy your students have. Remember y'all, teacher autonomy should lend itself to student autonomy. It's crucial that we reflect on our level of autonomy while simultaneously reflecting on our students' level of autonomy. Then I'll ask you to define it in practice. What specifically do you have autonomy over and what type of autonomy is this? And reflect on your feelings toward this. Get specific here. You may realize you have more autonomy than you think or you're actually satisfied. Lastly, if you don't have free autonomy, the unlimited power to make decisions for your students, then who does? Naming who is the gatekeeper of autonomy can help you to strategically target people you can have conversations with to gain more autonomy and support.

What do you have autonomy over as a teacher?

Is it none, taken, partial, or free? Is it a mixture?	Who controls what you have autonomy over?	How comfortable are you with this situation?

What do students have autonomy over?

Is it none, taken, partial, or free? Is it a mixture?	Who controls what students have autonomy over?	How comfortable are you with this situation?

What does autonomy mean to you?

BIG QUESTIONS: What is the role of autonomy in our profession? How does it look in your school?

Now it's time to think about the a-word, *autonomy*. First, start by crafting your own definition. I learned through dozens of interviews that teachers have their own definitions. Starting with a foundation will help you to navigate through the reflection. Then, reflect on your students' level of autonomy. Remember, adult autonomy should in turn give students autonomy. They are the center. Next, reflect on your own autonomy. This is most effective with your teacher team. It will help you to all be on the same page moving forward. From here, you can share trends, SMART goals (specific, measurable, achievable, relevant, time-bound) to address them, and action plans. You may find that you need more autonomy and choice in one area and more support and guidance in another. The conversation on autonomy should be ongoing.

TEACHER REFLECTIONS

Javin C., Chicago, Illinois
Ninth- to twelfth-grade English teacher, Assistant Principal
Years in the classroom: 5

Q: *What does **autonomy** mean to you?*

A: Autonomy means doing what I think is best for students and their trajectory. I was a high school English teacher. My job was to make sure they had the skills and concepts necessary to be adults. As freshmen in English, I know they're going to leave this space and need skills to navigate where they go: college, trade school, army, entrepreneurship etc. You need to have some basic knowledge like comprehension, communication, writing and critical thinking. Did I have that autonomy? No.

Q: *What do you have autonomy over?*

A: Daily lesson plans in our 10th-grade curriculum

Q: *Is it taken, partial, or free?*

A: Partial.

Q: *Who controls this?*

A: The English Department decides what books we read and the skill scope and sequence.

Q: *How comfortable are you with this?*

A: I didn't like the scope and sequence that was created. It doesn't work for 99 percent of the students we serve so I try to respond in ways I can.

We were reading *The Piano Lesson* by August Wilson. My students were living on the West Side of Chicago, and they had a very limited scope of music. My students were like "I don't understand the music being played and the music behind the story." "This doesn't fit our time. Can you help us gain some better understanding of this?" I responded quickly.

Three students stayed after school and we created this musical subunit to explain the times, the lyrics, and the sounds of that particular era. We wanted to bring other people in. We had someone bring their B3 Organ for students to gain an appreciation of the music during the 1930s. It was because students spoke up that I fought for that level of autonomy. It led to greater levels of thinking and sparked interest in a unit.

**Katie W., Leland, Mississippi, and Detroit, Michigan
Fourth- through seventh-grade ELA teacher, full-time graduate student
Years in the classroom: 7**

Q: *What is the role of autonomy in our profession?*

A: When I think of autonomy right off the bat, the mental image I get is the classroom space. It's the day in and day out. I am in my classroom. I am the one thinking and collaborating with students. There are other decision makers and systems influencing you. However, teaching by its nature is autonomous because it's very much a tango between you and the students.

Q: *How does it look in your school? What does autonomy mean to you?*

A: I had autonomy over content but not over organization and structure of my unit plans. As long as I ended up with a final project and a writing piece, I was fine. As long as I started each day with a daily learning target then I could fill in the blanks.

I need autonomy over content for sure. If you tell me to teach this book and I'm not jazzed about it, students will know in a second. To give a very specific example one of my students said, "Why do I keep seeing TikToks about colonization and we never talk about how colonization impacts us?" Another student told me, "We never talk about Native Americans." She kept bringing that up. Autonomy means being able to respond to student content needs and questions. I want to have some autonomy and flexibility if students bring something up that I can address.

Sometimes your direct boss isn't the one who gets to make the decision. It's someone in the district office who has to rubber-stamp it and all those layers mean less relationship and less knowledge of the classroom. When you don't have a relationship there is a lack of trust. There is too much distance between the decision maker and the teacher.

CHAPTER FIVE

A SLOW-MOVING TRAIN

Patrick, Not Pat :)
@PresidentPat

Fighting for change in schools is tough. Whether you're an administrator or teacher. Changing the mind of adults is hard work. Through relationship building, strong delivery, and purposeful planning, leadership and change can happen.

Jan 29, 2019

IN MY SECOND YEAR OF TEACHING, I TAUGHT FIRST GRADE. OUR SCHOOL WAS ON THE 40/40 list—a public list of forty of the lowest performing schools impacting forty communities. My school's goal was to improve literacy scores, and the primary method of achieving this was doubling down on the district's mandate to fuse five components of literacy into a 120-minute balanced literacy block in grades K–2, daily: phonics, close reading, guided reading, independent reading, and reading centers with a computer reading program. Like many large-scale plans, it sounded great in theory. But in practice . . . boy oh boy. It was not easy.

Check this out. Half the team was second-year teachers and the other half was preparing for retirement. We all had varying levels of knowledge and expertise on the best ways to teach reading, phonics, and writing. As second-year teachers, we still had work and learning to do with crafting our teaching identities and gaining confidence to facilitate meaningful literacy instruction. And if that was not enough of a struggle, time was always of the essence. If you're not in education, setting aside 120 minutes may sound like an ample amount of time. But every educator knows how quickly time flies when you have nineteen first graders in a classroom, when the announcements take a little longer than usual, or when our students' humanity takes center stage. Still, every minute mattered. From the moment my six-year-olds walked into the room, the pressure was on to check every box in the literacy program while staying on schedule. Not one minute over or under. Each transition was timed and rehearsed.

As professionals, perfectionism beats us up day after day. My team and I were all comfortable teaching one part of the literacy block and struggled in another, leaving us feeling incomplete. I loved teaching close reading and I was successful at it. But I struggled to teach guided reading. My students could tell. We would spend extra time with close reading while guided reading was rushed. And my administration stated this ultimately had an impact on my students' first literacy assessments. We expressed the need for training and guidance. And deep down, we were not fully bought into this system. We had a different idea.

In the midst of our school's midday professional development, we began asking the right questions at the right time. "Is there another way we can implement this literacy block?" Someone transposed the question into "How can we be innovative and still meet the demands of the district?" The literacy coach showed us she was on our side when she said, "You know. Wait a minute. I heard there was another school doing something different." Our ears leaned in. It's so easy as educators to get stuck in your school's quicksand. Change and innovation in schools feels impossible when you are a soldier of one. One school, one team, one classroom. In a school not far from us and not on the 40/40 list, they were implementing a successful literacy program in which teachers became experts in one component of the literacy block and taught it to the entire grade. To limit the number of big transitions,

> # CHANGE
> ## IS DEFINITELY
> ### GOING TO HAPPEN,
> NO MATTER WHAT WE PLAN OR EXPECT TO HOPE FOR
> ### OR SET IN PLACE.
> # WE WILL
> # ADAPT
> ### TO THAT CHANGE,
> OR WE WILL BECOME
> # IRRELEVANT.
> —ADRIENNE MAREE BROWN

teachers moved between classrooms and students benefited by learning from each teacher's strengths. We took on the task of adapting this.

Our small team met on a weekly basis, during our one planning period and after the final bell rang, to work through the kinks. What would this program mean for our students? How do we transition students? What will it mean for a kindergartner, for first and second graders, to have three literacy teachers instead of one? How would it impact their social–emotional learning?

After nearly a month of preparation, we felt confident in our plan and felt ready to pitch our pilot program to our administrative team. Our principal and assistant principal walked into the room smiling with excitement. "Alright now!" We described the pilot program in detail. To end our presentation, we shared our intention to spend more time over the summer, with our administrative team's support and resources, to further craft the program, pilot it in the fall, and reflect on the assessments to decide if it was making an impact.

The presentation ended in applause. We smiled and laughed, oozing "thank God it's over." The administration did not hold back in asking questions. "How would this work with transitions?" "What if there's a new teacher?" "How much money do you need for professional development?" and "Is this developmentally appropriate?" Though we were nervous, we bounced off of one another to answer all of their questions. We worked together and even leaned on our retirees and literacy coach for their expertise. Our administrative team looked at each other and then applauded us for our teacher leadership, innovation, and teamwork. They asked for a few days and said that they would get back to us.

And that was it. We waited and waited on an official response from our school administrators. On the last day of school, we still did not hear back. We sent follow-up emails after the school year ended and finally had a meeting with our administration team weeks after the last day of school.

The principal, vice principal, director of operations, and special education coordinator sat around a round table. The principal started by thanking us again for our leadership, creativity, and innovation. I knew where this was going. It was transitioning into the inevitable and elongated "Buuut . . ." That's when she passed out papers. She and the rest of the administration team had taken our plan and added annotations. It was essentially a list of ten reasons why our plan would not work. They cited scheduling issues, what's considered developmentally appropriate, and our standardized test scores. She spent the bulk of her speech saying that we needed time to become better teachers before we could do any sort of innovating. There was no invitation for a conversation or any sort of compromise. That was it. Imagine our faces. Forehead tight, brows coming together, eyes emotionless. What else was there to say? We lost. We thanked them for their time and left.

The next day, as I was leaving the school after picking up an item I left in my class-room, I ran into the vice principal. He asked if I was upset by the decision they made. I quickly replied "I was disappointed, not upset." He wanted to voice (again) his main concern: the schedule. "What about social studies? It's completely eradicated from the list." I wish I had better control of my visible irritation. My voice dropped an octave, "The district mandates thirty minutes a week. I think we can integrate social studies into close reading because we're pressed for time." There was a beat. He thought about it. And a minute later doubled down on policies, protocols, and expec-tations from the central office. I pushed back again, young and confident and a tad bit cocky. "How can we support our students, not the people in central office?" He had the final say. "Humble yourself. You've only been teaching one year. You need to have a few more years before you can challenge me." Final kill. The next week, I submitted my resignation.

Reflecting back, I realize the plan was well thought out, but it had too much room for error. Our administration was under immense pressure and was not willing to take a risk on innovation because the weight of eradicating the 40/40 status from the school's name laid on their shoulders. My resignation came not because I was hurt from our plan being denied, but because the administrative team created barriers to change that seemed too tall for us to climb. The resistance was not about loopholes or best practice; as a second-year teacher I felt a lack of trust and belief in us. And I convinced myself that there was no way I would be able to make change in that environment.

My understanding of change has evolved over the years. My current beliefs are a sum of my experiences in several schools and the ways I have reframed them using my belief in emergent strategy by adrienne maree brown. At its core, emergent strategy is a practical philosophy for doing complex social justice work, rooted in simple beliefs of relationship, trust, and small action (brown 2017, 22–23). She shares that change is as natural as the elements. (There's a reason why trees last for hundreds of years.) We must see through the depths of our shared humanity and begin to move in harmony. In order to make the sustainable change in social justice work, she has taught that sustainable change happens when we understand how interconnected we all are. Us. We.

To sustain myself in the profession, I had to process my own beliefs about change. I know I'm not alone with having an unspeakable frustration with the ways our country and systems leave the needs of children and teachers out to dry. I have a witness out there? Our frustration with the system is one of the biggest reasons why teachers quit and a part of this is a misunderstanding of how change happens. I want you here for the long haul. So it can be helpful to examine what happened through the lens of emergent strategy.

Informed by brown's core principles, here are my beliefs about change in schools:

> *Effective change is slow and small.*
>
> *Change is about relationships, not just about strategy.*
>
> *Change reveals our interconnectedness.*
>
> *Systems of power are upheld by people.*
>
> *Change is constant.*

EFFECTIVE CHANGE IS SLOW AND SMALL.

I label myself a fantast. This means I am a dreamer. I ask myself big questions that I don't have the answers to. I think of big plans that some people raise their eyebrows in "I don't know about all that" energy. My solutions are usually just as big as my dreams and my questions.

Just burn it all down and start over. I mean, that's the easiest way right? But I have learned through failure, through conversations, and through relationships that dreaming big means thinking small. Brown teaches us that small change is still a reflection of the larger system. As cheesy as it sounds, planting the seed still matters.

WHAT HAPPENED?	WHAT I BELIEVED ABOUT CHANGE	WHAT I BELIEVE NOW (AS INFORMED BY EMERGENT STRATEGY)
My team and I wanted to completely overhaul and replace what was in place immediately.	Change happens when we dream big and take risks for our students.	Small change is slow, but it is still change. The ways we are able to start small still impact the larger system because they are interconnected.
Our grade level team had brainstorming meetings and put together a presentation for our administration .	Change happens best when we work with those who are next to us. Including our administration in these conversations would not have been helpful since they are the gatekeepers.	Change happens best when we decentralize leadership positions. When we all can come to the table as equal partners in the work, we can build relationships that lead to change. There is no need for gatekeepers when we are all equally invested.
Our administration team told us that we needed to be better teachers before we could make change.	There is a disconnect between principals and teachers. All schools should eradicate principals and other top-down leadership positions that take power away from school teachers.	It felt like a disconnect between teachers and principals because the stakes are too high and the trust was too low. We were not moving at the speed of trust.
Our administration team was under immense pressure to get off the 40/40 list.	Administrators, who are often the gatekeepers of radical change, wanted to keep up the status quo.	We are all interconnected. And affirming our interconnectedness comes from empathy. The small risks we take in our schools impact all stakeholders.
My principal told me, "You are only a second year teacher. You can't challenge me."	Teachers have to continue to fight against administrators in order to move forward.	Systems of power are run by people. Find the value of spreading decision making power to everyone, but especially students.
The administrative team shutdown our plan.	If it does not happen at this moment, change is impossible.	Change is slow but it is constant. And every plan, conversation and risk we have contributes to change in a small way. Restrategize, work on trust, keep going.

So, that risk you take in your classroom still counts. Developing a plan even though it does not get adopted still matters. Organizing a protest and a list of demands still counts. Scheduling a meeting to build a connection still counts. Change, particularly in schools, is slow and it starts small. This is because everyone wants buy-in. And in theory this is a good thing. We cannot make change without having us all onboard. (Beware of those with privilege and power who purposefully block change.) When we start small, this can still lead to big change. You may not be the one who waters the seed or feeds it or ensures it gets sunlight on cloudy days. But, roses, even in concrete, don't grow without seeds.

CHANGE IS ABOUT RELATIONSHIPS, NOT JUST ABOUT STRATEGY.

This is layered. From my experience, I have learned that making change in school is hardly ever about how good your plan is. You can spend all day and all night dotting your i's and crossing your t's. Include the latest research. But if you do not have the relationships with the people who the change will impact, it is useless. Relationships in education are measured by trust. It took me a long time to learn this. I used to think my administrators, colleagues, students had to "like" me. You know what I mean? Being liked is a temporary feeling and it is something you hardly have any control over. People's personal roller coasters will impact whether they like you today and whether that changes tomorrow. But trust is more long-lasting. Trust is measurable. Trust is something you can plan for. You feel me? And so, while I may not always like my administrators, I have to figure out if I can trust them to make the best decisions for the students and educators in the building. And they have to know they can trust you. I know ego, perfectionism, and pressure can be in the way. Emergent strategy pushed me to think about animals and plants and how they trust without debate. I saw an Instagram reel recently that showcased a colony of bees making a ball around an imposter queen bee. She had to be destroyed. Without question, argument, or debate these bees worked together to create a ball around this sus bee. They buzzed in harmony creating a pocket of heat. This heat exploded

WE ARE EVERLASTING DEBTORS
TO KNOWN AND UNKNOWN
MEN AND WOMEN.
WE DO NOT FINISH BREAKFAST
WITHOUT BEING DEPENDENT ON
MORE THAN HALF OF THE WORLD
. . . AT THE TABLE WE DRINK
COFFEE THAT IS PROVIDED
FOR US BY A SOUTH AMERICAN,
OR TEA BY A CHINESE,
OR COCOA BY A WEST AFRICAN.
BEFORE WE LEAVE FOR OUR JOBS
WE ARE BEHOLDEN TO MORE THAN
HALF THE WORLD.
—MARTIN LUTHER KING JR.

the bee into bits and then the colony of bees went back to protecting their actual queen. Nothing would stop them from protecting their ecosystem.

As humans, particularly adults, we do not work well together unless we have a certain level of trust. (This is what we mean when we say buy-in.) And rightfully so. History has taught us to not trust each other because humans create unnecessary harm every day. Whether physical, emotional, or mental violence, institutional violence or educational violence, our flawed nature makes room for distrust. But if we are moving towards change, trust is a very necessary component. This requires intentionality and risk-taking. Self-awareness and evaluation. We must be intentional about building trust with our students and their families. And our colleagues and administrators. We must respect that this trust takes time, depending on the person. But that's OK. Change is small and slow. Trust also requires risk-taking. Sometimes we are in the building stages of developing a relationship or a relationship is rocky. We can still choose to trust one another. In some cases, we have to choose to trust one another. Give the plan a chance, even if you think it may fail. Allow colleagues and administrators to voice their opinions; it may push the conversation forward. If we don't trust people, we can't build relationships. And without relationships, change is impossible.

This also means knowing and engaging with opposing views. Now let me be clear here. Our country glorifies extremists. I'm not talking about them: white supremacists, Karens, obstructionists. Not them. I'm talking about people who have a different experience than you and simply disagree with your ideas (not your humanity). In grad school, I learned that algorithms are designed to show you ads and posts you are likely to engage with. And studies show that you are likely to engage with posts that affirm your own beliefs. Thus, as much time as we spend on our phones giving our opinions, it is less likely that we are actually having healthy dialogue with people who disagree with us. I choose to believe that we all have the same end goal in education: to prepare heathy and whole young people to thrive in the world. But we all have different ways of getting there. It is our duty and responsibility to affirm our shared humanity and give space to have dialogue.

CHANGE REVEALS OUR INTERCONNECTEDNESS.

Change is often coupled with fear. *How will this impact me?* The more we discuss change in schools, the more we reveal how connected we all are. What we do as teachers impacts our administrators. The activities we plan impact custodial staff. Deciding to renovate a building impacts the surrounding community. The laws and policies created by local school boards impact teachers. And all of the ways we make decisions in education impact young people. Period.

An easy way to think about interconnectedness is to consider the way the building shifts when someone is absent. You know that feeling when you come in and the hallway is quieter than normal. Or when you go down to pick up your class for the start of the day and you see a substitute. "They're not here today?" You may acknowledge a shift in your energy. This is showing how interconnected we all are.

So when we are considering the ways we can make change, we have to consider how everyone is impacted by that change. Remember, we want to make systemic change because it's long-lasting. And if we are changing systems, then we must know that everyone is impacted by this. As we are devising our plans, it is healthy for us to acknowledge the ways our interconnectedness will be impacted by change.

With this interconnectedness, we should see the value of interdependence and shared leadership.

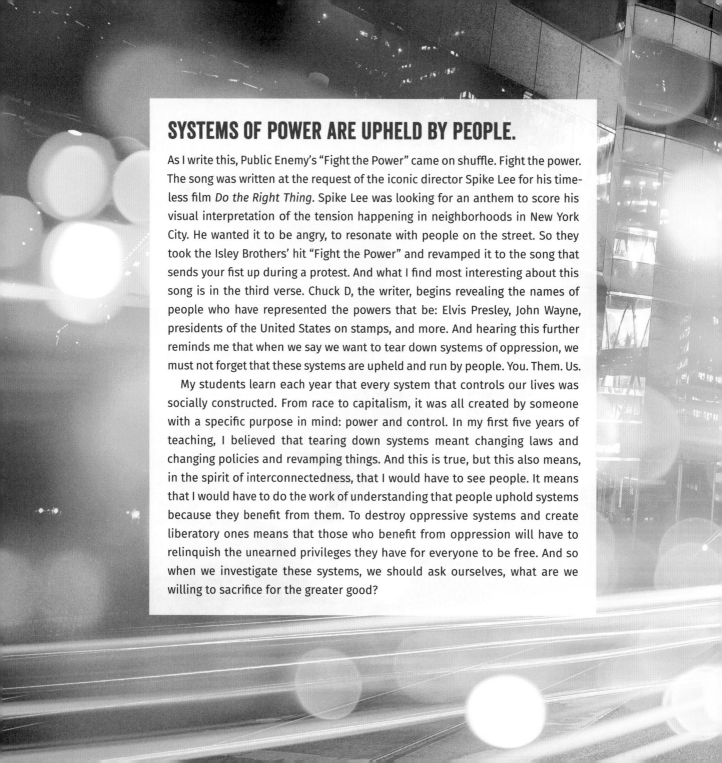

SYSTEMS OF POWER ARE UPHELD BY PEOPLE.

As I write this, Public Enemy's "Fight the Power" came on shuffle. Fight the power. The song was written at the request of the iconic director Spike Lee for his time-less film *Do the Right Thing*. Spike Lee was looking for an anthem to score his visual interpretation of the tension happening in neighborhoods in New York City. He wanted it to be angry, to resonate with people on the street. So they took the Isley Brothers' hit "Fight the Power" and revamped it to the song that sends your fist up during a protest. And what I find most interesting about this song is in the third verse. Chuck D, the writer, begins revealing the names of people who have represented the powers that be: Elvis Presley, John Wayne, presidents of the United States on stamps, and more. And hearing this further reminds me that when we say we want to tear down systems of oppression, we must not forget that these systems are upheld and run by people. You. Them. Us.

My students learn each year that every system that controls our lives was socially constructed. From race to capitalism, it was all created by someone with a specific purpose in mind: power and control. In my first five years of teaching, I believed that tearing down systems meant changing laws and changing policies and revamping things. And this is true, but this also means, in the spirit of interconnectedness, that I would have to see people. It means that I would have to do the work of understanding that people uphold systems because they benefit from them. To destroy oppressive systems and create liberatory ones means that those who benefit from oppression will have to relinquish the unearned privileges they have for everyone to be free. And so when we investigate these systems, we should ask ourselves, what are we willing to sacrifice for the greater good?

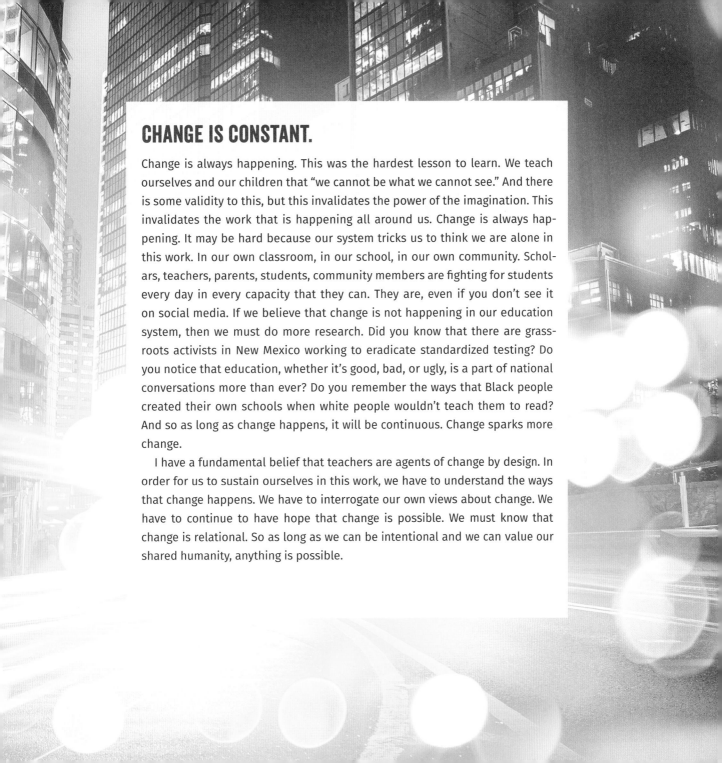

CHANGE IS CONSTANT.

Change is always happening. This was the hardest lesson to learn. We teach ourselves and our children that "we cannot be what we cannot see." And there is some validity to this, but this invalidates the power of the imagination. This invalidates the work that is happening all around us. Change is always happening. It may be hard because our system tricks us to think we are alone in this work. In our own classroom, in our school, in our own community. Scholars, teachers, parents, students, community members are fighting for students every day in every capacity that they can. They are, even if you don't see it on social media. If we believe that change is not happening in our education system, then we must do more research. Did you know that there are grassroots activists in New Mexico working to eradicate standardized testing? Do you notice that education, whether it's good, bad, or ugly, is a part of national conversations more than ever? Do you remember the ways that Black people created their own schools when white people wouldn't teach them to read? And so as long as change happens, it will be continuous. Change sparks more change.

I have a fundamental belief that teachers are agents of change by design. In order for us to sustain ourselves in this work, we have to understand the ways that change happens. We have to interrogate our own views about change. We have to continue to have hope that change is possible. We must know that change is relational. So as long as we can be intentional and we can value our shared humanity, anything is possible.

BIG QUESTION: What is the key to unlocking radical change in our schools?

Alright, buckle up. Let's talk change. I want to help you prepare to make a small change in your context, action research style.

Let's start here:

Through the eyes of a student, what barriers are they facing to learning? To being themselves?

Through the eyes of a faculty member, what barriers are you facing to teaching? To being? What barriers are your colleagues facing? Do you see any trends?

What changes have your school or district made in the last year? Five years? Twenty years? Who has been centered in these changes?

Alright, let's dream big!

What does an ideal solution look like? What impact will that have on you? Your students? Your school? Your community?

What does a short-term solution look like? What do long-term solutions look like?

Uh oh! Let's take a pause.

If you propose your ideal solution, what barriers might try and stop you? Are they systemic? Are they people?

Who's in your support group? Working with people can really help you to move the needle faster. The more you diversify your support group with different stakeholders, the more successful you can be.

What does patience look like?

Let's keep going!

What does a good short-term goal look like? What does a long-term goal look like?

When the opposers push against you, how will you push back? How will you support yourself?

TEACHER REFLECTIONS

Desmond W., Washington, DC
Former teacher, grades 3–7 special education
Years in the classroom: 9

Q: *What is the key to unlocking radical change in our schools?*

A: The key to unlocking radical change is asking how you get all our stakeholders to investigate the software in their head. We must know the software is there by default. It's just there. We are born into this education system, and people want to do what they experienced in schools. It's what they see as the "right" thing. Are we really going to do what we did when we were six? We have to convince ourselves that it is time to figure out how to switch gears.

When I think about that radical change, I think about asking ourselves what the current research says and determining with everyone how you bridge the gap between research and practice. How do you do it for all kids in this environment? How do we adjust to see if it still works, years later? Ultimately we have to get past our own egos and learn to self-evaluate. Small changes bring about big changes eventually.

We must also remember that our day-to-day interactions with our students bring about change. Our pedagogical practices bring about change. The research bears that out. It's about our students. They will always remember Mr. Harris for how he treated them not because of any dope lessons. They'll remember the love you gave them, the field trips you took, the way you helped them in the midst of a crisis. Plus, how are we preparing to embrace their multiple identities (cultural, sexual, gender, religious, racial) through the content we put in front of them and those identities and that content and making the world more just. We have a chance to meet students where they are every day, even when the system is not on our side.

Ngesihle Ingy M., Doha, Qatar; Pietermaritzburg, KwaZulu–Natal, South Africa
Kindergarten teacher
Years in the classroom: 4

Q: *Through the eyes of a student, what barriers are they facing to learning? To being themselves?*

A: I have not started school yet. What I do know is that we are given a scripted, preplanned curriculum for the entire year. We are not allowed to move away from this curriculum. This is what we do. Here are the lesson plans. Here is what we will do in the classroom. I can infer that my students will not get the whole benefit of what they should be experiencing in the classroom. Instead of getting an individualized experienced, it will be one-size-fits-all.

Q: *Alright, let's dream big! What does an ideal solution(s) look like? What impact will that have on you? Your students? Your school? Your community?*

A: Ultimately, (1) I want to come together with other teachers to discuss regularly how we can create, implement, or change the current curriculum. (2) I want to be able to create new things that reflect my students because as the world changes, we also have to change and adapt. (3) I would like to attend regular trainings on curriculum development and leadership.

I think the students will have a more personalized experience in the classroom. We will adapt to them as opposed to them having to change for us.

If this happens, I will feel more confident teaching my students. It will help me to be a better facilitator of knowledge. And I would also be able to collaborate with my own students. My autonomy will trickle down to them. In turn, they will feel more confidence because they will know I do not have all the answers. We are working together. As I was growing up, I did not have a voice in my own classroom. I was told what to do and how to learn by my teachers. I don't want my students to have the same experience.

Q: *What does a short-term solution look like? What do long-term solutions look like?*

A: A short-term solution would look like having a building conversation with the people in charge. Those are not always easy. But when you start to have those conversations, it starts to build trust. I know I have not started at this school yet, but I want them to get to know me.

A long-term solution would look like a protocol for collaboration with our curriculum.

CHAPTER SIX

FACTS OVER FICTION

 Patrick, Not Pat :)
@PresidentPat

My experience teaching abroad has been anything but glamorous. Lots of tears, headaches, and moments of hopelessness. I'm still unsure if I'm going to make it. But, these last two days (my colleagues and my students) have ignited my optimism.

Jan 11, 2019

I DID NOT REALIZE THE SEVERITY OF MY DECISION UNTIL THE PILOT SAID, "PREPARE FOR takeoff." Freshly fired with nothing but $300 in my pocket, I was tucked tightly in the rear of the plane. My forehead resting lightly on the windowpane, I watched the last of the luggage get stowed away. It did not take long before the plane began using all its weight to push itself back. There is no turning back now. Everything I had ever known and loved faded into the skies.

I accepted a year 6 (also known as fifth-grade self-contained) international teaching position in Doha, Qatar. When you say it that way, it sounds cool. But in context, a Black boy from the East Side of 7 Mile in Detroit, Michigan, packed his bags and went to teach elementary school in the middle of the academic year 6,000 miles away from home. I'm the first in my family to attend and graduate a four-year university. I was the first in my family to pack my bags and enter in a career outside of the state of Michigan. And I was soon to be the first in my family to live internationally.

I arrived in Doha around midnight more than a day later. When you step off the plane and walk into the overpass, the heat hits you. It's dry and harsh, like standing in front of an open oven. The heat was no match for the air-conditioning in the Hamad International Airport. My eyes were met by bright fluorescent lights and my feet landed on marble floors. I stood in the immigration line for nearly an hour. My immigration officer was stoic. He used very few words. I looked into a machine, a robot if you will, on the side of the kiosk. The machine jolted up and down, checking to see if I appeared to be the real Patrick. He affirmed that I was not just passing through. I had a one-way flight. I had as many clothes as I could fit into one checked bag. I carried as many school supplies as possible to have a successful year: pencils, paper, base ten blocks, a few read-aloud staples, and a WWE wrestling belt. A few stamps into a passport and I was officially an expat. This was home.

"Welcome to Doha!" a man said with as much excitement as he could muster at midnight. I was in Qatar, but this man looked nothing like anyone I would meet in Qatar. Before I could inquire, he smiled and said, "Let's get you settled." Everything began moving fast. He took me to the phone booth to purchase a SIM card. "You can put this into your phone." (This ended up not working.) Next, he took me to the currency exchange. I exchanged the last $300 USD to my name into Qatari Riyals. Finally, he guided me out of the airport and back into the heat. He put my suitcase into the back of a large white van decorated with hand-painted blonde hair and blue-eyed kids, smiling bright. I was feeling the exact opposite.

"Are you excited about being here?" He asked me in an unfamiliar accent.

"I think so," I hesitantly responded. I wanted to say yes. I desperately wanted to say yes.

Fresh from being released from my dream school, only twenty-six years old and having the opportunity to be halfway around the world, I should be excited to start over. But I was unsure. My driver was the human resources director and originally from the Philippines. He had worked at the school for several years. The most tedious part of his job was coordinating the travel of incoming teachers. I was curious why he chose Qatar as a place to live. He says there are many Filipino expats in Qatar; it is a place of opportunity. It is a chance to make money to send home to his family.

We departed the airport and drove into the future. The architecture of Doha is light years ahead of Detroit and DC. The buildings were anything but typical. In the dark of night, they flickered pinks, purples, and greens. They were cone-shaped; they twisted and turned at sharp angles. I was not home anymore. Not far from the intergalactic skyline, I arrived at my apartment building. We put a long skeleton key into the door revealing a small three-bedroom apartment. The school provided me all the things I would need to get settled: housing, groceries, furniture. I did not have to pay a dime for any of it.

Despite being so unsure, my aura screamed "expert." In my short years as a teacher, I've learned teaching requires a level of confidence even in times of uncertainty. Our profession does not allow us the grace to be uncertain, to struggle, to fail. Time is always of the essence. We don't have the time to be anything but perfect. If teachers are off our A game, our students suffer, which means our schools suffer and as a consequence our communities suffer. My fear of activating the chain of suffering continued because I was serving in Black communities. "The work" weighs heavy on our shoulders. Being international, being a United States of America–born, Black, male,

queer, international teacher on top of that added an extra layer. Being an American, I was already seen as more qualified than those who were certified South African teachers or who had years of experience teaching in the Philippines. And my own functioning anxiety stemming from perfectionism was the icing on the cake. I started teaching only twenty-four hours after arriving in Doha. My ideas around education, and particularly what it meant to listen and build relationships, would be challenged.

Before my alarm clock could ring, I was woken by the sound of prayer. A deep, vigorous prayer, in Arabic. A little over twenty-four hours later, I got up at 6:00 a.m. Doha time (about 8:00 p.m. EST) to prepare for school. I wore gray slacks, a baby blue button-up, and a chromatic striped tie. In addition to the professional wear, I wore fear loud and clear. It was in my eyes. Adrienne Waller, a Black woman from Detroit who went to my same high school, asked if she could pick me up for the first day of school. On our commute, it was eighty-five degrees and the air was dusty. Behind the clouds of dust, I could make out the futuristic skyline from the night before.

After a few roundabouts, left and right turns, we arrived to what looked like a sandcastle. The school was gated in a neighborhood. Walking up to the gate, passing through sand and dust, the school resembled a small village. Hand-painted beige buildings sat on Doha's version of grass: green turf. I was accompanied into the main building. It echoed. There were many nationalities represented in the staff of the school. The principal was a man from the United Kingdom. The assistant principal was a woman from Lebanon. The teaching staff were predominantly teachers from South Africa and Ireland. The assistant teachers and support staff were all from the Philippines. Adrienne, the school's instructional coach, and I were the lone staff members from the United States.

Similar to home, I was the only Black male teacher in the building. Some things aren't so different. The school principal welcomed me. He gave me a brief tour of the main building, asked me how I felt. I replied nonchalantly, "OK." They walked me over to the building where my classroom was. I opened the door to my room. I was in someone else's classroom. The walls were plastered with student work. Twenty-seven desks of a variety of colors, stained with drawings, were carefully placed in rows. He told me I could plug my laptop into the projector hanging from the ceiling. He told me to not worry about instruction, they would train me on the British National Curriculum soon. And then he said, "Good luck" and closed the door behind him. I wish I could make this up. I did not even know where the bathroom was.

Before I could catch my breath: a *knock knock knock*. I opened the door to three of my students. They all wore long plaid skirts and the white, short-sleeved shirt with the school logo on the right-hand side. They each had a black satchel with the same embroidered unicorn on it. Their skin was brown and their hair was long. They did not

speak, but they waved and took seats in the front of the classroom, speaking amongst themselves. One beat later, a group of boys were outside of the room, switching between Arabic and English. "A new teacher" was all I could make out. Before I could go outside and greet them, the horn sounded and the hallways were now crowded with students walking towards the large open "grass" field. It was 7:00 a.m. and the temperature creeped up to 93 degrees.

I stood awkwardly on the side watching them go through their school tradition. I had a clipboard in my hand for show. They began with the Qatar National Anthem. All of the students sang from their guts, especially the kindergartners. The principal welcomed everyone back from their holiday breaks. Students stood in single file lines with their teachers at the head. The student body of 500 ranged from kindergarten to fifth grade. They represented several nationalities in the Eastern hemisphere: Qatari, Sudanese, Egyptian, Iraqi, and more. The skin tones varied across the student body, some olive, tan, sun-kissed, and midnight. The melanin was of abundance and I found comfort in this. I identified as Black before anything else, and I knew I would be able to find common ground to build relationships.

After our all-school assembly, I walked behind my students as they led me back into the classroom. It was now just me and them. Before I could speak a word, my students snickered and said things I could not understand. My stomach churned, but "fake it till you make it."

"Hello! My name is Patrick Harris. You can call me Mr. Patrick" (this was a part of their school culture). I awkwardly blurted out, "I'm American." Isn't that how you

Patrick, Not Pat :)
@PresidentPat

I think I've really struggled to build and sustain relationships over the year. Today, I'm giving my own teacher "report card," that I give to my students every year. I'm just wondering if it's as bad as it was in my head.

May 28, 2019

introduce yourself at international schools? Their eyes widened. This was the first time I had ever identified myself only as American. Typically, I am quick to identify as a Black male teacher, leaving the darkness of America on the side. But I didn't have to, my students did that for me. Over the course of the week, students from across the grades outwardly showed their curiosity for my Blackness. How could I be from America and be Black? It did not take them long to come to their own conclusion.

"Mister, are you the Kiki man!" I would hear this faintly as I walked my students to the playground for recess. Sometimes I resisted the urge to muster up all the rhythm I had to do the dance and other times I tried to stop myself from slicing them in two with my eyes. While I enjoy being compared to the looks of Drake, I found most interesting just how far Black culture can reach. We have the power through music, dance, and social media to shape the way the world sees and interprets Black culture. This is the power of art. In the same breath, I had an internal conflict every time a kid walked past me and said, "Kiki, do you love me?" and laughed with his friends. In their innocence, they were finding a way to connect with the foreignness in front of them.

On the playground, a kid said, "Mister, why do Black people always wear gold chains?" I responded swiftly with "Well, that's just the way we like to express ourselves," showing him my gold chain underneath my collared shirt. Seeing as though I'm from the richest country in the world, I didn't think the flashiness that can come with Black culture would be something to bring up. He told me I should give it away because gold chains and jewelry are only worn by women or people going to hell. I took my chain off, tucked it inside of my pocket. I told him, dangling it in front of him, that it is not like that in my culture. He told me I can give it away to any of the girls here. I decided not to choose this battle. I walked away.

Another kid asked, "Mister, do you want to be white?" White supremacy has followed me 6,000 miles away from home. I followed it up without hesitation, "Never." He

matched my confidence and told me that I should. He put his thumb on his forehead and said, "You can be born again." What in the Jim Crow is going on here? I made it perfectly clear that being Black is something I thoroughly enjoy. But I was only met with resistance from this student and his friends who believed that being white is better than being Black. But I just wondered why this was even a discussion in a country where racism, or so I believed, was not relevant (in the same ways I was used to). Being asked to erase my Blackness with the quickness of a thumb to the head by an eleven-year-old was the most traumatizing moment yet.

These are children. Just as human as I am. They are sponges that soak in what's available to them and spew it out when they feel comfortable enough to do so. I think they were using their relationship with me to ask all the questions they had and say all the things they've thought. This is the beauty and the headache of teaching while Black at an international school. There's so much difference and students are making sense of it in their own ways. I don't fault them for how they made me feel. But I do know that these constant comments made me gag. It gave me the timber to build barriers between me and my students. And the walls became so tall and so thick that I could not hear them.

While my students were exploring and testing me, I was under immense pressure by my school to begin thinking about accreditation. We were the only school in our network to not pass the Ministry of Education's accreditation test. This meant all eyes were on the teachers to gather documentation, to begin mastering routines, and to push ourselves to be "better." Accreditation coaching sessions took place randomly with representatives from the Ministry of Education. The pressure was on.

The casual racist banter and the accreditation pressure led me to stop listening to my students and just teach them; my classroom was out of control. It was not unusual for students to be disengaged from the lessons I taught. Despite the many activities I tried to pull together and the theories I had read, I came to the conclusion that my students just did not like me and being Black was the main reason. That was it. Why else would my students be late to class? Why else would my students speak to each other in Arabic in the midst of a lecture or class discussion? Why else would I engage in screaming matches with my students in an attempt to gain respect? We tangoed in this struggle all year, stepping back and forth between power and positivity.

As the year was coming to a close, I questioned whether I wanted to continue my tradition of teacher report cards. In an attempt to level the playing field in the classroom, I've always told students that if I'm giving them a formal report, then it's only right and fair that they give me one as well. The report card is a list of behaviors that students "grade" me on. I ask them what they have learned throughout the course of the year, how I could improve, and what things I've done well. The document is two pages long. The first page asks students to provide a "grade" on how I show up in the classroom. The questions are centered around care, their safety, and the relevancy of the content in our classroom. On the back, students are asked to write their key takeaways. It's good to know what students remember: what assignments resonate, what objectives stick, and whether students learn something completely different than what you intended. Overall, the report card is a great way to formalize listening to students. I went back and forth, wondering whether I needed physical proof of what I already knew. Adrienne said I should give it anyway and she would facilitate the process.

I was too nervous to even look at the reports when they came back. I pushed the folder of reports back to her. "You look at them first." She opened the folder and flipped through them one by one. The first thing she said was, "Well, they indeed knew that you cared about them. Everyone marked that as a 1." Ugh. The tears. I could not hold back the ugly sob that followed. She said how much they enjoyed my class. They said they had learned confidence and bravery. They

MR. HARRIS' REPORT CARD

I really value your voice and feedback. This is how we grow in community with one another. Remember, this is OUR classroom. I am asking for your honesty in evaluating key competencies that impact our class. Review the criteria and give your honest score.

1 = Mr. Harris is excellent at this. He shows the particular action often.

2 = Mr. Harris is good at this. He shows this particular action most times.

3 = Mr. Harris needs some improvement in this. He is inconsistent in these actions.

4 = Mr. Harris needs severe improvement and help in this. He almost never does this action.

	1	2	3	4
1. Mr. Harris shows me that he cares about me as a person.				
2. Mr. Harris has high expectations for me. He expects my best at all times.				
3. Mr. Harris teaches things that matter to me.				
4. The things that we learn in Mr. Harris' class I can use in my next school or in my next English class.				
5. Mr. Harris is fair when he gives consequences.				
6. Mr. Harris recognizes my hard work and praises me when I do something well.				
7. Mr. Harris grades my assignments fairly.				
8. Mr. Harris is enthusiastic when teaching, professional, and takes his job seriously.				
9. Mr. Harris makes learning fun.				
10. Mr. Harris listens to me and answers my questions thoroughly.				
11. Mr. Harris' class is challenging to me.				
12. Mr. Harris' classroom is a place where I feel safe.				
13. Mr. Harris is available when I need to talk with him about academic or personal matters.				
14. Mr. Harris presents information and class material in a way I can understand.				

1) What are three things you have learned so far in English?

2) What's one thing you wished were different about our class?

3) What is one suggestion I should take to be a better teacher?

4) Any additional comments?

learned perseverance. This was in addition to "maths" and "reading." Several surveys did not stray away from the conflict between me and my students. They said that too often I spoke too fast. EspeciallywhenIwasmodelingorgivingdirections. Oftentimes, they did not know what to do and pushed back when I would react to them "not listening." I sobbed.

I had told myself fiction for the entire six months. Rightfully so. Looking back, I will not excuse the feelings I had throughout this particular school year. I was a third-year, midyear, Black queer male teacher, teaching 6,000 miles away from home abruptly. I was deeply homesick, experiencing depression and anxiety. I dealt with microaggressions and hopelessness. There was so much clouding my judgment. I had so much happening to me that I did not take time to get the truth from my students. I kept seeking professional development, advice from colleagues, thoughts from Twitter. I talked to everyone except my own students about how to move our own class forward. They were right in front of me and I made them invisible.

Building relationships with students is something we do at the beginning of the year, but the work does not end here. After we build the relationship, we have to sustain and strengthen it. This is the work. Strengthening relationships with students is an ongoing process, not an objective on a checklist. It requires intentionality throughout the year. It takes reflection and apologies. It's not something that disappears as the curriculum and standards and testing take priority. Teaching is human work. The ways in which we strengthen relationships, the opportunities we create to truly listen to our students, can help us to make the best decisions as educators.

You do not have to travel 6,000 miles away from home before you begin listening to your students. I know as teachers, as human beings, we walk into our classrooms with bias and emotions. These should not be ignored. We are not robots. We have gut feelings that cause us to react. When we are working with students, it's important that we know the facts. Do we know why we feel the way we do? Do we know why students are reacting in these ways? Answering these questions requires deep self-awareness. I built walls brick by brick using false narratives I created in my head. Using rash, yet valid emotions. Seeking feedback from my students, understanding their needs, concerns, and thoughts gave me a sense of peace and closure. If any stakeholder needs our grace, our understanding and our ear, it's our students.

We must find ways to challenge traditional power structures that silence children. It's not your classroom. It's not their classroom, either. The space that you and your students create together belongs to everyone equally. And at the same time, we must recognize the power that we hold as adults, as teachers in schools. With power comes the responsibility to decentralize the power dynamic.

This means having a clear understanding of how your students feel, what they're experiencing, and their thoughts around the classroom (or school) community. Their feedback can help you feel more whole and make the learning experience more impactful for everyone.

You know why we are in this work. You know why we step foot in the classroom. It's our students. Sometimes I call them my kids. Understand that they walk into the classroom with strengths. They speak multiple languages; they have persevered through tough times. They are smarter than you in some cases. Make room. Get out of their way. Allow them the space to be, to grow, to fail. This starts with listening. Make room.

BIG QUESTION: What is the impact of de-centralizing the power dynamic between teachers and students?

As you are thinking about moving beyond building relationships and into strengthening relationships with students, it's important to always start inward. Before we talk about students, let's talk about you. Give yourself permission to check in with yourself. Start by answering these questions alone first. Then, if you're around folks you feel comfortable and safe with, share with them.

1. How are you today? What's happening in your personal or professional journey that helps you to strengthen relationships with students? What can cloud your vision?

After checking in with yourself, you can assess your classroom. This is best done in partnership with whomever you work with. If that's a coteacher, team teachers, SPED teachers, or grade-level leads, bring them in! It's also helpful to ask students their thoughts.

2. How do you measure the relationships between you and your students?
3. How do you create opportunities to listen to students? How often do these activities happen?

If you need a place to start, I have included the teacher report card I use for my students. Feel free to take it and modify it and allow students to give you feedback.

TEACHER REFLECTIONS

Melissa G., Washington, DC
First-grade teacher
Years in education: 7

Q: *What is the impact of decentralizing the power dynamic between teachers and students?*

A: It levels the playing field. It creates a strong foundation for human-to-human interaction. Not adult-to-child interaction. We forget that we have humans in front of us. Not just children. They are impressionable. They are curious and have different personalities. It is important to decentralize power dynamics between children and adults so children can feel space in *our* space.

We don't just take care of our house. We take care of each other. I tell them you may call me auntie, mama, cousin, Ms. Griffith, Ms. Melissa. None of the content or the lessons will matter. What do they remember? What do they walk away with? They understand. And they see what's going on.

Q: *How are you today? What's happening in your personal or professional journey that helps or hinders your ability to listen to students?*

A: My school was experiencing too much change and too quickly. Professionally, my school had lost its charter and was forced to close. So the following year our school had been taken over by the local public school. This meant new administration. Our new principal recently won "Principal of the Year," coming in replacing 50 percent of our school's staff with teachers from their old school. This change in management and administration created tension between staff members who were new and returning. Our school's culture was shifting towards "Got Ya" culture: lots of walk throughs and evaluations but not a lot of relationships being built along the way. And when you least expect it, admin walks in your room with clipboards to check what you're doing right and wrong.

Due to the charter being taken, the school had an awful reputation in the education system. Thus our school was put in a pressure cooker to turn it around or risk being shut down for good.

I was twenty-nine years old and completely struggling. Because the pressure was on me, I put the pressure on my kids. I felt helpless in many cases. So the one thing I could control were my students. I upheld power dynamics between me and my students.

Q: *How do you currently measure the relationships between you and your students?*

A: We had lots of check-ins. Especially after recess. I would stop teaching and we would just have conversations about what was going on and see how they felt. This happened consistently and pushed me to adjust my teaching. I measured the relationship by how they showed up to the class every single day. Feeling the pulse of the room.

Q: *Knowing this, how can you create opportunities to listen to students? How often can these activities take place?*

A: We eventually started integrating SEL lessons. We learned a lot about empathy and that is what flipped the switch. Everyday we read passages that had vocabulary words missing. I had them fill in the blank. So they were working on a reading skill and we were listening to each other, discussing social issues that mattered to them. But it was through the lens of safety and culture. We also established regular journaling: a safe place for them to check in with themselves and me. They could tell me anything and did. They did goal setting for themselves, not for me. When we established a routine together, it became a place where they wanted to be. This began to spill into our lessons. They began working harder, being unafraid to fail because it was a safe space to do so.

Adrienne M. Waller, Cayman Islands
(Has also taught in Chicago, Detroit, Qatar, China, Kuwait)
Assistant principal and small business owner
First- through fifth-grade teacher
Years in the classroom: 10

Q: *What is the impact of decentralizing the power dynamic between teachers and students?*

A: It's like a pitcher of water. There's only so much space in the pitcher. It's not endless. The more I pour water into the jar, the less space for students. And also, students are sharing space with other students. Kids are vying for space. As you reduce your space, students get more space, more chance to live out who they are and discover who they are. They're young and in the midst of discovering themselves. As you move out, they can move in.

Q: *How are you today? What's happening in your personal or professional journey that helps you to strengthen relationships with students? What can cloud your vision?*

A: At this time I'm in a relationship. My first out-of-college real relationship. But we're having some issues. I'm trying to figure out a place that I want to be. How do I speak up for what I need while fighting for a relationship? I am trying to figure out my educator voice. I did a lot of shifting. I was at a bunch of different schools. Is this where I'm supposed to be? And it's OK to disagree with the person on the other side—my principal. They don't understand me right now. They told me to stop coming to them for every little thing. I did not understand that I was not in the hood. But I'm in a new school. In my educator space, I started having mentors at the school. They were encouraging and helping me. I am questioning if I still want to be in the profession. This is not going well. Having my mentors as a sounding board is helpful. But I don't have it in my personal space.

I had an inverse relationship. As I wasn't getting fulfillment in my own relationship, I dug into more of my kids. I would be one of the last teachers in school and the first to be there. Maybe I wasn't putting as much effort into the relationship as I put it into my kids. I couldn't get something in my relationship so I nurtured it in my classroom. Some of this was unhealthy. I fed Ms. Waller and not Adrienne. I had a parent who volunteered biweekly. My parent brought me dinner after work, on late nights, when I would stay late and do work. I wondered why I was not at home eating dinner with my partner or how often I was waking up early to come to school, neglecting [my partner].

Q: *How do you measure the relationships between you and your students?*

A: One way and it's super informal: I did a lot of conferencing about everything. We did wellness check-ins. Informally. I would talk to the kids. One thing is that I had fabulous relationships with parents and parents always gave feedback. I sent home surveys with parents. I wish I had formalized that feedback process a lot more. Google Forms and Sheets were not out yet!

Q: *How do you create opportunities to listen to students? How often do these activities happen?*

A: In a one-on-one setting, I listened to my students daily. I also did morning meetings and class talks. We had biweekly afternoon time and just chatted. Kids had an opportunity to share what was working and what was not working. Thumbs up or thumbs down. I was one-on-one with a set of kids every day. Most of my check-ins were content related but I also made sure to check in with their humanity.

I made myself available beyond just class. I ate lunch with kids and went to music class at least once a semester. I also went to birthday parties, recitals, a grandfather's birthday party, soccer games. I was heavily present in these different spaces and I opened up my own room.

CHAPTER SEVEN

AND WHAT ABOUT ME?

Patrick, Not Pat :)
@PresidentPat

Sometimes, as a teacher who teaches the "hard stuff," I worry about my classroom feeling too heavy too often. To combat that feeling, I tell myself and sometimes my students if we're tired of reading + learning about it, imagine living it daily. The content is necessary.

Jan 6, 2021

JANUARY 6, 2021

Thousands of angry pro-Trump supporters from across the country gathered for a rally in our nation's capital. They were enraged by the announcement that Donald J. Trump would only serve one term after losing to Joe Biden in the 2020 presidential election. Through conservative algorithms used by journalists, social media influencers, and elected officials, lies circulating Trump's false claim that the election was stolen were fed to his supporters, leaving them full of rage.

The rage pushed thousands of supporters, including teachers and educators, over the edge and into the streets of the nation's capital. They answered Trump's call to protest the election results and interrupt the certification of Joe Biden as our forty-sixth president and Kamala Harris as our first Black and female vice president. While they were in the streets, I was on my couch in the midst of remote learning. This was our school's flex day, which meant I had more downtime than usual to catch up on work and watch the news. In the beginning, I felt desensitized to the anger. We had been through four years of dangerous words and rallies. I had no shock to give. Unlike what I learned in schools, the racist rhetoric being spewed at this rally did not come from people wearing white sheets or masks. They were ordinary Americans. Loud and proud and angry. Confederate flags would fly back and forth. The American flag would be stomped and burned. I could see the red rising. When Donald Trump empowered his base with chants and cheers and a call to action: march to the United States Capitol to "fight back." I chuckled in disbelief. He has said something crazy again.

Before I had a moment to adjust, the mob began stampeding down the street without organization or civility—just wrath. Within minutes and without major opposition, they stormed the United States of America's Capitol. They clobbered windows and slithered through the front door of America's symbol of democracy.

It was a horror movie. The mob infiltrated the floors of the Senate and the House of Representatives with ease. They rushed and ransacked the private offices of our elected officials, vandalizing everything in sight. Members were hiding behind locked doors, fearing for their lives underneath wood tables. There were children present. This was no kindergarten tornado drill. This was indeed a classic terror attack: an unorganized, chaotic incident that seemed to have no actual plan but to bring fear to your living rooms. They knew, amid a pandemic, you'd be watching. A siren of terror.

Our democracy was being attacked.

What I thought was just another public, attention-seeking temper tantrum evolved into an insurrection. We were in the midst of a middle school faculty meeting when the insurrectionists breezed past the first barricade of cops. I was unable to focus on our school's upcoming schedule. And, if I'm being 100 percent real, it was a camera-off, mute, speaker-off type of moment. My jaw was on the floor.

While people just saw this as an attack on our government and our democracy, I also saw it as an attack on my former students in Washington, DC, where I began my teaching career and taught for four years. Some of my students' parents worked at or near the Capitol in a variety of roles. This was not just an attack on a system; it was a physical attack on people and residents.

While my colleagues in the meeting were responding to the current events with one another, I was shell-shocked. Unable to move. I was watching news commentators

Patrick, Not Pat :)
@PresidentPat

The beginning of this documentary really reminds me as an educator that every second and every decision counts for children. It could truly make all the difference. What if they didn't suspend him for those two weeks? #TrayvonMartinStory

Jul 30, 2018

refer to the armed people climbing the walls of the Capitol as protestors. They faced hardly any military opposition and were able to enter the Capitol with ease. Even in the midst of our country being attacked on a global stage, the media still gave them grace.

The insurrection was triggering. My gut was filled with grief for all of the Black people that I had watched be murdered by law enforcement in real time. My heart sank to my feet for all of the names who would not get national publicity. I ached for all of the Black people who were killed and still await their justice. For Trayvon Martin. For Mike Brown. For Sandra Bland. For George Floyd. For Freddie Gray. For Rekia Boyd. For Breonna Taylor. And too many more.

I was filled with unspeakable rage when I recalled the treatment of those who filled the streets to tell the world that Black lives matter. When I helped to organize a die-in for Mike Brown in college, we were called expletives by those who "disagreed." When Baltimore youth threw rocks at police officers after boiling over in response to Freddie Gray, former President Barack Obama said there was "no excuse for violence" from these "criminals and thugs." Before protestors even had the opportunity to assemble after the killing of Freddie Gray and Breonna Taylor, mayors set citywide curfews and allowed police officers to show up in militarized gear holding automatic weapons. I saw tear gas being thrown into crowds. I saw the wounds of rubber bullets up close. I saw the kidnapping of protesters into unmarked cars live on television. The way police officers treated Black Lives Matter protestors and our collective response to grief was criminal. And yet, a large mob, at the direction of the former president of the United States, was able to break into the United States Capitol during a historic joint session. With no immediate consequence.

We know Black Lives Matter protesters would not have been allowed to break down a barrier of police to the United States Capitol, let alone break windows to climb inside or vandalize the Senate floor or make their way into the office of the Speaker of the House, breaking down doors sending staffers and their children to hide. That could not have happened. Well, I'll say that it would not have happened because it's not something that Black Lives Matter protesters see as effective, necessary, or healthy for our country. It's not how we organize.

I was no longer desensitized. All of the grief, the anger, the hurt, the disbelief hit me at the same time. I had spent years being desensitized to the ways Black people and protesters had been treated. Our media has been saturated with anti-Black content.

This moment in our history reminded me I had seen varying levels of white supremacy before. I had been exposed to white supremacist rallies since elementary school. As a kid, I remember seeing the KKK burn crosses in cartoons and documentaries during Black History Month. I remember hearing stories of hangings from my grandparents. I have seen modern-day pro-gun and pro-white rallies across this country. But there was something different about the January 6 insurrection: I finally cried. Years and years of rage. Of frustration. Of hopelessness. I could not hold back my tears any longer. "Why am I crying?" I asked myself. It was the weight of the COVID-19 pandemic, amplifying every emotion all the time. It was fear of what would happen next. More importantly, I was finally allowing myself a chance to feel all of my humanity.

Whew. The tears were flowing. As the military showed up and insurrectionists gave in, social media put the pressure on teachers. The hot question was, how would teachers talk about what is happening at the insurrection in their classrooms the very next morning? If this was Patrick in his first year of teaching, without question, I would have been gathering resources, coming up with questions, activities to add to my lesson plan the next day. I felt this way after the Parkland shootings. After Breonna Taylor's murder and the brutal protests that followed. After the 2016 election. And the California wildfires (and the prisoners they use as free labor). If it was all over the news, then my students *had* to be thinking deeply about it or wanted to talk about it. I needed to prepare myself to talk about it straightaway. I often used current events as a way to throw scripted curriculum to the side and engage my students in learning that was more relevant. But, insurrection on the Capitol was different. Instead of wondering how I would organize the lesson for the next day, I was thinking about taking the next day off. This shift was new.

Patrick, Not Pat :)
@PresidentPat

Do I teach about this tomorrow or do I take off? That's really the question . . .

Jan 6, 2021

MOST FRUSTRATING FOR CRENSHAW HAS BEEN WATCHING THE GOP REDUCE **CRITICAL RACE THEORY** TO A CUDGEL TO ATTACK PROGRESS IN THE GUISE OF **PROTECTING DEMOCRACY.** 'IN THE SAME WAY THAT **ANTI-RACISM IS FRAMED** AS RACISM, **ANTI-INDOCTRINATION IS FRAMED AS INDOCTRINATION,'** CRENSHAW SAYS. — *VANITY FAIR* MAGAZINE

The shift in my thinking was partially a response to the context in which I taught. I was a sixth- and seventh-grade humanities teacher who taught at a gifted, tuition-based, independent school about twenty-five minutes north of Detroit, in the city of Birmingham, the wealthiest city in the state of Michigan. My students were predominantly white, and I was in some cases some of my students' first Black or first Black male teacher. Though we had a positive classroom and school culture, I was traumatized by the horror in DC. And I was unsure, in my state of shock, if I was emotionally ready to "teach" this current event the very next day (even if it was remotely). I knew at this point I needed to rest and give myself time to process what was still unfolding.

Too often, as teachers, we are asked to put the pressure on ourselves and sacrifice our own needs for the needs of our institutions. Too often we are asked to put our well-being on the sideline to endure emotional labor. Too often we are asked to teach about traumatizing events before we have offered ourselves enough time to process and heal from them. Culturally responsive teaching and teaching for social justice are very popular but so are misconceptions about what they mean: many educators believe they mean overexposing our children to traumatizing content in the classroom, without any real regard to our or their emotional well-being. We have to release ourselves from the pressure to address traumatizing current events.

At the time I'm writing this book, thirty-three Black trans women have been murdered. But teachers are not held accountable for talking about this in the same way we are held accountable for talking about white violence. What our society deems as urgent to discuss in classrooms is rooted in cisgender heteronormative privilege and white supremacy.

Before we talk about how to address emotionally charged and traumatizing events in our country, whether current or historical, we need to check in with ourselves. We have to affirm the emotions that we feel deep inside. We have to acknowledge the work that we have to do before we talk about how we bring this to students. Remember, teaching is human work. This means journaling. This may look like getting on the phone with people you love—calling your family, your best

friends, folks online that you haven't met before. It may mean booking an appointment with a therapist. For me it looks like all of that and then also an impromptu teams call with my colleagues. And we didn't call to talk about what we needed to do with students. We just gave each other space to process. To cry and breathe audibly. We gave each other time to be human.

We are still in the midst of a pandemic. COVID-19 has swept through our education system, exposing the trauma our systems have put us through to the world. And in many cases, amplified the stressors that we endure on a daily basis. Surveys funded by the National Education Association (NEA) and American Federation of Teachers (AFT) found that more than three in four teachers reported frequent job-related stress. A report from *Edweek* shared that teachers were also "more likely to report experiencing symptoms of depression than the general population" (Will 2021). There are still false narratives that circulate the internet that claim teachers have it easy. Our working conditions say otherwise. Going years being severely underpaid says otherwise. The ways we were forced to take the entire country online with minimal training and support but high expectations say otherwise. In addition, we must endure the world events that happen on a daily basis and walk our students through them.

I made a decision to go into work the next day. But I did not teach. The next morning I gave students a choice. I put together a list of readings and articles, and I told my students over the screen that while we cannot ignore the events that happened yesterday, we should not skip the individual reflection time each of us needs. I gave my students an asynchronous day of learning. They could choose to stay logged onto the call and read independently. They could discuss their emotions with each other. They could also completely log off and practice self-care. It was completely up to them. They knew that I would be there in whatever capacity they needed me. But I needed not to be leading any conversations at that moment. I knew at that moment I needed time to process. I knew at that moment I needed to put myself and my own needs first without apology.

In addition, our middle school team offered a town hall meeting for four hours where students and faculty were allowed to just come and talk and process their feelings. In a structured and safe space, students rattled off frustrations and questions. Some students logged on and listened.

Faculty members offered their commentary not as experts but as human beings who needed time and space to process. Occasionally, we would provide some historical context. But, the town hall brought us together as one community.

The insurrection on January 6 also led to a discussion on social media around the role of teachers. People believed that those who broke into the Capitol must have had teachers who did not do their job. They must have missed several days at school when this should have been addressed. They must not have mastered the standards or misunderstood the content. And thus, teachers should feel the pressure to discuss current events in class so that they do not pass along the next extremist. I reject this narrative with everything in me. We are not always in a space to facilitate meaningful conversation about current events with students, so we should not force it. It assumes that all teachers tell the truth and teach through an anti-racist lens and prepare students to fight against white supremacy. We do not. Educators were amongst the insurrectionists on January 6. Currently, dozens of states across the country have taken action against discussing racism (with the support of some educators) in schools. It assumes that schools and

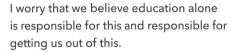

Patrick, Not Pat :)
@PresidentPat

I worry that we believe education alone is responsible for this and responsible for getting us out of this.

At some point, you all will have to understand that schools are not solely responsible for the shaping of a person. Schools are merely a reflection of our society.

Nick Covington
@CovingtonEDU

I worry about our ability to teach our way out of this. Are we really asking the right questions about the ends & means that will get us there?

Put bluntly, what standards do we imagine these people missed?

What about education is an inoculation against white supremacy?

Jan 10, 2021

FROM STARFISH, I HAVE LEARNED THAT IF **WE KEEP OUR CORE** INTACT, WE CAN REGENERATE. **WE CAN FALL APART,** LOSE LIMBS AND RE-GROW THEM AS LONG AS WE DON'T LET **ANYONE THREATEN THAT** CENTRAL DISC'S INTEGRITY. *WE* CAN GROW SO MANY DIFFERENT ARMS, **DEPENDING ON WHAT KIND OF SEA STAR WE ARE.** WE HAVE TO NOURISH OURSELVES WITH THE RESOURCES WE **ARE SURROUNDED BY,** WITH OUR COMMUNITY ASSETS IF YOU WILL AND BY DOING **SO WE HELP KEEP [OUR] ECOSYSTEM** DELICATELY BALANCED. —JOLILLIAN T. ZWERDLING

educators are solely responsible to address violent white supremacy and any other social ill in our society.

White supremacy and systems of oppression were not born in school. Educational institutions are merely a reflection of what happens outside of the school walls. We see how oppressive institutions and systemic issues seep their way into school buildings and create challenges before we can even ring the first bell. We know that to make a difference in the lives of our children, it takes all hands on deck. Schools and educators cannot fix societal issues alone. We all have to take accountability and responsibility for how society has shaped those who have attacked the Capitol. Those who reject the idea that Black lives matter. Those who constantly advocate against the rights of LGBTQIA+ people. Those who violently assault and kill Black trans women. That's not just on schools.

And that's not to say that current events and tough issues should not be talked about in schools or integrated into curriculum. That's not to say that what we do say in schools doesn't matter. It is certainly the responsibility of schools to ensure that we have a safe place for all students to process what is currently happening in our world, as they are living through history. That's crucial. However, we should ensure that we have had time to sit with what's happening, that we have had the time to do our work on current events before we can execute a meaningful lesson plan. We don't want to retraumatize students or ourselves because we weren't ready. If we are not ready to have academic lesson plans to process information, it is OK to just hold space for students to get their thoughts off their chest. Then we must ensure that the adults in the building have conversations with one another first. If it's an issue of racism or sexism or any other discrimination that dehumanizes a human being, we as adults should take time to process and honor our humanity. We are not superheroes or robots. We are humans. We are human beings that feel, that grieve, that get angry.

WHAT IS THE EVENT?

How are you feeling? What are your gut reactions?	What does this event remind you of? What does it bring up for you?	What does this mean for how you navigate your personal or professional life?
What does this mean for your students?	What does this mean for your community?	Do you need to address this right away? Can it wait?

BIG QUESTION: How can teachers honor their humanity as they feel pressure to respond to current events?

On the previous page, I've included a reflection tool you can use to process a current event. It will help you to dive deep into your own work. The questions I will ask you will be personal to you. It might be best to answer these alone, unless you have someone near you that you trust to be vulnerable with. Then I will ask you what your reflections mean for your teaching.

You can brainstorm a plan of action that will be most beneficial for you and your students. The planning document works best in teams. The more adults can be on the same page, the better it is for students.

TEACHER REFLECTIONS

Deion J., Orangeburg and Greenville, South Carolina
Seventh- through tenth-grade English
Years in the classroom: 5

Some days we intend to teach but reality takes over. In the midst of a lesson, there was a lockdown. This was not on the schedule for the day. The kids and I were frantic. What's going on? We were instructed to wait until we got a knock on our door. And so we sat in our room, waiting for a knock on our door, trying not to overwhelm ourselves with such little information. *Knock knock.* A police officer came to our door and asked everyone to leave. All of our bags would be searched. We left our belongings in the classroom. In the hallway, we were all antsy, trying to put two and two together. Then the officer came out of the classroom with one of my student's book bags and said, "Whose is this?" One of my students brought a gun to school.

My class and I were forever changed by that moment. We all witnessed him being taken by the police officer, never to return for the remainder of the school year.

After the search, we were told to continue with our lesson. I asked myself how do I address what just happened? I still have my students in this period. In that moment, I had heightened anxiety. In my head I was struggling with an internal battle, putting the pressure on myself to make a decision and fast. Do I have a conversation with my students against my administrator's wishes? Do I establish a sense of normalcy and not cause any disruption? Or is it already disrupted?

I stopped. I think I needed time to feel the room and see where my students were. The side conversations and their expressions told me that they were freaked out. And so in response, I did what I thought was best, which was to continue on with a sense of normalcy to attempt to relieve tension.

At that time, I felt my job was not to facilitate an academic discussion around what was going on. Instead, it was to focus on the well-being of my students. Let's just continue on. But they had their own agenda. At first, it was an act of resistance. They were so anxious to talk about the things they just witnessed. But I pushed back against them. I knew I did not have the tools to talk about it. I was still figuring out what just happened myself. As the time passed, my class started to become chaotic with fear and utter shock. I calmed the class and settled us back into our routine. I thought it was best at this point for everyone to just continue as normal.

Eric W., Mississippi Delta
Eighth-grade middle school language arts, writing,
and public speaking teacher
Years taught in the classroom: 14

The year was 2019. A very popular football star had come out as gay. In the city of Boston, there was a straight pride parade. In response to the parade, Jidenna, a popular musical artist, came out against homophobia in Africa.

I allowed students to discuss whether LGBTQIA+ history should be taught in schools. I did not want to teach a full lesson, but I just wanted to do a quick check-in. I knew they were thinking about it. Some students shared, "I don't believe in gay contributions. Their histories don't deserve to be taught." I followed up with, "Should Black history be taught in schools? Should women's history be taught in schools?" Some students joined the pushback saying, "Black people are overlooked in history. The same can be said about women. Can the same be said for the LGBT community?" I was just facilitating the conversation. It sparked so much dialogue about our own experiences. They took ownership over their opinions, sharing that their thoughts and feelings surrounding queer folks were passed down from their parents. At the end of class, we had a stronger understanding of inclusion.

I identify as a Black bisexual man. In my own personal experiences I have learned growing up in the south to take time to learn my own triggers. Always always always make sure that you understand your triggers when you come to these controversial topics. I'm sensitive to them. I've heard teachers say they want to address controversial topics but take a defensive attitude to anything triggering a child, who is new to having these types of conversations. Is it the child or is it you? Where is the trigger coming from? We have to know our triggers, work through them. Then we can stand in front of students. I knew entering this particular conversation, I had to keep in mind that they are children first. They have room to grow, they have more to be exposed to.

Ironically, the following week, our school called a staff meeting to alert everyone that we had a student who identified as transgendered. The principal wanted us to know that the school will take on a zero tolerance policy for bullying. "We don't want to cause attention. Be diligent when it comes to children. If you see something, say something. Automatic suspension." As big of a deal as the adults were making, the students were just fine. It was the adults who were snickering and making comments on her clothes, shoes and questioning her masculinity. I was disappointed. I was at an IB school. These were teachers who were required to teach international issues. It was a great opportunity to model how we should behave and act when these things happen. Trans kids are kids. They're like everybody else. It should not be a big melee. Adults need to have deeper conversations with each other about our beliefs instead of just worrying about the children. With a safe space to grapple with issues and talk, the kids are alright.

WORKS CITED

Adelman, Larry. 2003. *Race: The Power of an Illusion*. California Newsreel.

American Psychological Association. n.d. "Autonomy." *APA Dictionary of Psychology*. Retrieved October 1, 2021. https://dictionary.apa.org/autonomy.

Archambault, Leanna, Catharyn Shelton, and Lauren McArthur Harris. 2021. "Teachers Beware and Vet with Care: Online Educational Marketplaces." *Phi Delta Kappan* 102 (8): 40–44. https://doi.org/10.1177/00317217211013937.

Bailey, Marlon M. 2013. *Butch Queens Up in Pumps*. Ann Arbor: University of Michigan Press.

brown, adrienne maree. 2017. *Emergent Strategy: Shaping Change, Changing Worlds*. Reprint ed. Chico, CA: AK Press.

Eastern Connecticut State University. 2021. "Columbia Professor Encourages 'The Archaeology of Self' to End Racism." February 21. https://www.easternct.edu/news/_stories-and-releases/2021/02-february/columbia-professor-encourages-the-archaeology-of-self-to-end-racism.html.

Emdin, Christopher. 2021. *Ratchetdemic*. Boston: Beacon Press.

Foster, Michelle. 1997. *Black Teachers on Teaching*. New York: New Press.

GLSEN. n.d. "LGBTQ Educators: What We Know and What They Need." Retrieved October 6, 2021. https://www.glsen.org/blog/lgbtq-educators-what-we-know-and-what-they-need.

Grinnell College. n.d. "Underground Ball Culture." https://haenfler.sites.grinnell.edu/subcultures-and-scenes/underground-ball-culture/.

Grow, Kory. 2014. "Riot on the Set: How Public Enemy Crafted the Anthem 'Fight the Power.'" *Rolling Stone*, June 30. https://www.rollingstone.com/feature/riot -on-the-set-how-public-enemy-crafted-the-anthem-fight-the-power-244152/.

HUD Office of Policy Development and Research (PD&R). 2000. "SOCDS Census Data: Output for Southfield City, MI." https://socds.huduser.gov/Census /race.odb?msacitylist=2160.0*2600074900*0.0&metro=msa&frames=$frames$.

Johns Hopkins University. 2018. "Black Students Who Have One Black Teacher More Likely to Go to College." November 12. https://releases.jhu.edu/2018/11/12 /black-students-who-have-one-black-teacher-more-likely-to-go-to-college/.

Jones, Jeffrey M. 2021. "LGBT Identification Rises to 5.6% in Latest U.S. Estimate." Gallup.com. August 13. https://news.gallup.com/poll/329708/lgbt -identification-rises-latest-estimate.aspx.

Kincaid, Jamaica. 1978. "Girl." *New Yorker*, June 19. https://www.newyorker.com /magazine/1978/06/26/girl.

Learning Policy Institute. 2017a. "Teacher Turnover: Why It Matters and What We Can Do About It." August 16. https://learningpolicyinstitute.org/product /teacher-turnover-brief.

———. 2017b. "What's the Cost of Teacher Turnover?" September 13. https://learningpolicyinstitute.org/product/the-cost-of-teacher-turnover.

National Center for Education Statistics. 2015. "Teacher Turnover: Stayers, Movers, and Leavers." Condition of Education. Updated November. https://nces.ed .gov/programs/coe/indicator/slc.

Montessori, Maria. 2008. *The Montessori Method*. Scotts Valley, CA: CreateSpace Independent Publishing.

Omokha, Rita. 2021. "How Critical Race Theory Mastermind Kimberlé Crenshaw Is Weathering the Culture Wars." *Vanity Fair*, July 29. https://www.vanityfair.com /news/2021/07/how-critical-race-theory-mastermind-kimberle-crenshaw -is-weathering-the-culture-wars.

Shakur, Tupac. 1999. "The Rose That Grew from Concrete." In *The Rose That Grew from Concrete*. New York: Pocket Books.

Strauss, Valerie. 2015. "Black Male Teachers: There Aren't Enough of Them." *Washington Post*, April 28. https://www.washingtonpost.com/news/answer-sheet /wp/2015/04/28/black-male-teachers-there-arent-enough-of-them/.

Vilson, Jose. 2020. "Some Remainders from the 'Moving from Equality to Equity and Justice' Workshop for NCTM." April 29. https://thejosevilson.com/some -remainders-from-the-moving-from-equality-to-equity-and-justice -workshop-for-nctm/.

Will, Madeline. 2021. "Teachers Are More Likely to Experience Depression Symptoms Than Other Adults." *Education Week*, June 15. https://www.edweek.org /teaching-learning/teachers-are-more-likely-to-experience-depression -symptoms-than-other-adults/2021/06.